THE BLESSINGS
ALREADY ARE

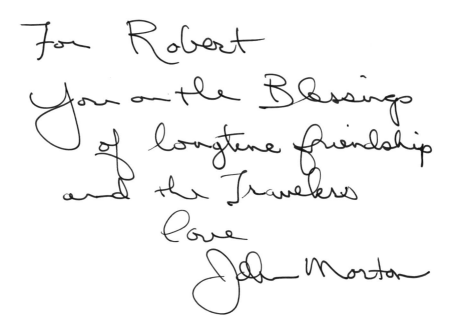

For Robert

You are the Blessings
of longtime friendship
and the Travelers

love

John Morton

OTHER WORKS BY JOHN MORTON

Are You Willing to Be God? (audio)
Attunement to God (video with Laren Bright)
Being Human and Spiritual (video with Laren Bright)
Blessings, Prayers & Invocations (audio)
Dream Journeys (audio read by John Morton)
Dreams, Wayshowers and Natural Knowing (video with Laren Bright)
Everyday Soul (audio & video with Laren Bright)
Gathering of Peacemakers (audio with Leigh Taylor-Young)
How Can We Follow Christ? (English/Spanish) (audio)
In the Line of the Traveler (English/Portuguese) (audio & video)
Inner Worlds of Meditation (audio with John-Roger)
     Introduction to Meditation & Spiritual Exercises
     Flame Meditation
     Meditation of the Color Rays of Light
     Water Meditation
The Law of Cause and Effect (video with Laren Bright)
Letting You In (audio)
Light & Sound, A Children's Story (audio read by John Morton)
Living a Necessary Life (audio & video with Laren Bright)
Moments of Peace—Sending Light and Peace Around the Planet (video with John-Roger)
Money: The Great Mirror of Consciousness (audio with John-Roger)
     In God We Trust
     Seeding for the Harvest
Money: The Great Mirror of Consciousness (video)
PAT V Seminars and Meditations (audio & video)
PAT V (audio with John-Roger)
     What Makes a Marriage?
     Listening for the Lord
Playing a Round with God (video)
Responsibility (video with Laren Bright)
The Season of Harvest (audio)
Solving Here and Now (video with Laren Bright)
Who Am I? (video with Laren Bright)

For more information, please contact:
MSIA®
P.O. Box 513935
Los Angeles, CA 90051-1935
323/737-4055
soul@msia.org   www.msia.org   www.theblessings.org

The Blessings Already Are

John Morton

Mandeville Press
Los Angeles, California

Published by Mandeville Press
P.O. Box 513935
Los Angeles, California 90051-1935
323/737-4055
jmbooks@msia.org
www.mandevillepress.org
www.theblessings.org

Printed in the United States of America
ISBN 0-914829-67-X
10 09 08 07 06 05 04 03 02 01 00   CR   10 9 8 7 6 5 4 3 2

Library of Congress Catalog Card Number: 99-64180

Our thanks to the following who allowed their works to appear in this book:

Quotes from THE PROPHET by Kahlil Gibran
Copyright 1923 by Kahlil Gibran and renewed 1951 by
Administrators C T A of Kahlil Gibran Estate and Mary G. Gibran
Reprinted by permission of Alfred A. Knopf, Inc.

Quotes from THE KABIR BOOK by Robert W. Bly
Reprinted by permission of Beacon Press © 1971

Quotes from THE ESSENTIAL RUMI translations by Coleman Barks with John Moyne
Reprinted by permission of Threshold Books © 1995

Rumi quote translated into Farsi by calligraphers Nasser Marghzar and Siamak Marghzar
Assistance with Farsi quote: Siamak and Tomi Jean Yaghmai
Interpretation: Mehdi Sarreshtehdári
Calligraphy: Nasser Marghzar and Siamak Marghzar

To John-Roger

CONTENTS

viii

FOREWORD

I N 1978, A QUIET, unassuming young man showed up at my door and declared that he was here to work with me and to dedicate his life to the Spirit. He looked earnest and sincere, and I saw, in the way I have for looking at things, that he meant what he said. At least, he meant it at the moment.

Since the work I do is pretty much 24 hours a day, seven days a week, I thought we'd just see how long this dedication would last. It has lasted a long time. So long, in fact, that I identified him as one of my heroes and role models for my book, *Spiritual Warrior: The Art of Spiritual Living.*

I think part of the reason John Morton's devotion to the work of demonstrating Spirit's presence has stood the test of time is because of his unswerving devotion to the God of his heart and his willingness to see the blessings in every moment. Amidst life's challenges, this is a very admirable quality and one I would encourage every person to develop and nurture.

When John told me he was writing a book about the blessings in life, I thought, "How appropriate," because I have observed in John a unique ability to impart the essence of blessings through his words. In my experience, each time John delivers a blessing, the Spirit comes present in a very tangible way. This is a rare gift. And that John has decided to share it in this beautiful book makes it a gift to you and all who will read it.

As with any manifestation of the Spirit, it is a two-way street: The Spirit presents Itself, and there is a measure of responsibility on the part of the recipient to place himself or herself in a position to receive. So, when you read this book, I challenge you to move past the beauty of its design, move beyond the words, and open yourself to receive the essence of what is present. There are profound messages in these writings. What's more, there is a profoundly uplifting experience available through them.

I know that what is in these pages has come from John's heart. I hope you will open your heart and receive it with all the love that John has put into it.

John Morton has been one of the blessings in my life. Through this book, may he become one of the blessings in yours.

Baruch Bashan.
JOHN-ROGER

x

INTRODUCTION

I HAVE FOUND THAT THE DEEPEST, most meaningful aspects to my life are often the ones that first appear to be so ordinary and inconsequential. The source of the blessings in my life is deep within, past whatever abilities or attainments I have or don't have, past any circumstances or fortune, past whatever can be seen as a cause or an effect. That source is still invisible and unknown and yet the most real aspect of my life. Praise be to God.

My desire to know that Source, to know God, has led me to know that the blessings of God, the changes for greatest good, already are present even when unseen and unmanifest. The immediacy of blessings has led me to convey my experience to you in this book. In the Bible we are told, "Seek ye first the kingdom of God, and his righteousness; and all things shall be added unto you."[1] And so I consider my seeking of God and the goodness that is the

---

1. Matthew 6:33

essence to be the key to realizing the blessings and all that is true.

As I was moving toward graduation from college in 1972, I had the notion that I should know what I was going to be doing with my life, some sort of life plan identifying my career path, where I would go, and who I would primarily share it with. I didn't know, and, thankfully, I knew that I needed to realize a few things about who I am before further embarking on my chosen life path. But what I needed to know or even how to go about it or who to contact was most perplexing. And so I searched, and I prayed to someone or something I didn't know outwardly. I trusted that whoever I was praying to would truly know and somehow would lead me or come to me with answers.

In 1974, a fellow park ranger told me about a spiritual awareness seminar he was attending. I knew in that moment that I was onto my answer. That knowing led me to John-Roger and the Movement of Spiritual Inner Awareness (MSIA), the primary resources not only for this book but for my livelihood and greatest blessings. John-Roger is my best friend, my teacher, and MSIA is where I live. I have endeavored to write directly from my experience, but clearly my experience is so infused with the teachings of John-Roger and MSIA that you may be better served to simply disregard this book and go there.

To have a true friend is one of the greatest blessings. My true friend and wife, Laura, continues to show me that the blessings of love are the greatest blessings, including our precious children, Claire, Zane, Mimi, and Max.

I have seen the blessings of perfection that led to this book, and truly everything and everyone have played a part, with some more than others. Many have encouraged me. And there are those who came forward to offer what I would not or could not do.

More friends. Judi Goldfader has been the head cheerleader leading the rally all along the way; she also happens to be a most capable publisher. Tom Boyer has been the chief instigator, providing the impetus so necessary to get off the ground. Lynn Vineyard toiled in the mines of what I have said here and there to unearth bins of material in the hopes that some gems might be found. Timothea Stewart plucked blessing upon blessing from the four corners, a task I'm sure she was born to do. Laren Bright has been the steady heart and sharp mind on refining the words on the page and putting the feet to the ground. Betsy Alexander has been my long-time mentor and crack copyeditor. Stede Barber, Shelley Noble, and David Sand have taken their considerable creative talents to make all things written look and feel good. Paul Kaye, MSIA President, along with his co-presidents Vincent Dupont and Mark Lurie have wholeheartedly footed the bill and provided the means to a blessed end.

The essence of all blessings is goodness. Let's go out and do some good.

JOHN MORTON
August 1999

An Invocation

❧ FATHER-MOTHER GOD, we call ourselves forward into the Light, giving thanks for your presence and for this opportunity to come together

    in your Spirit,

    in your trust,

    in your grace.

Give us your thankfulness, that we can know you are glad we are yours, that we may again put aside

    our doubts,

    our mistrusts,

    our fears.

We humbly come before you, open and naked, and we cast aside whatever would cover or keep us from you, so that we may be pure before you and have that sight of you.

So be it.

Baruch Bashan.

BARUCH BASHAN

I usually end my talks with "Baruch Bashan" (pronounced bay-roosh bay-shan). It is a statement that means "the blessings already are"—that blessings are present, and all we have to do is to partake of them, enjoy them, and appreciate them. That is what a genuine relationship with God and Spirit is really all about: The blessings of God are present and available.

"The veil that clouds your eyes shall be
   lifted by the hands that wove it,

And the clay that fills your ears shall be
   pierced by those fingers that kneaded it.

And you shall see

And you shall hear.

Yet you shall not deplore having known
   blindness, nor regret having been deaf.

For in that day you shall know the hidden
   purposes in all things,

And you shall bless darkness as you
   would bless light."

KAHLIL GIBRAN

Chapter One

THE BLESSING OF IT ALL

Consider this: If you were entirely loving, nothing would bother you.

I N THE WORK I DO—which is about knowing God as a living reality and supporting others into their own experience of that—there is a lot of focus on blessings. That's just the nature of the reality I inhabit. While this book is about the many blessings available to us in everyday life, there is an essence of ten blessings that infuses all the others. These are the blessings to which we are all entitled and which are available to all of us all the time if we have the eyes to see them.

John-Roger has identified these ten blessings as loving, caring, sharing, health, wealth, happiness, abundance, prosperity, riches, and touching. You will see elements of them in all the blessings throughout this book, so it seems appropriate to define these essential blessings here.

The first blessing is **loving.** There is always an opportunity to open up to greater loving. If you want to know what my work is about, the bottom line is that it is about loving. **If you are invoking and evoking your loving nature, it will lead you into the highest consciousness.**

Loving is the opening. It is the portal. All pass in loving. All enter through loving.

Consider this: If you were entirely loving, nothing would bother you. Maybe you've experienced that at times. When the force of love, the power of love, is completely open and emanating, there is an ecstatic relationship to everything. Everything sets you into your greatest sense of who you are and what your life is. Isn't that a great place to be? Well, wherever you find yourself, you can use your power of creativity, your volition, to choose loving.

The second blessing is **caring.** That blessing is an expression of loving. It's how loving makes itself known. It is a consciousness that allows another—and yourself— to be received in love. That's the consciousness of caring: It embraces through love, it touches in love, it speaks in love.

Simply put, caring is the consciousness to make things better, to extend yourself so things are lifted and are left better than you found them. That is the consciousness of caring in motion. We all have the power to choose to be caring so that our record as a consciousness will be one of caring.

Sharing is an interesting blessing. As we come into the power of who we truly are, we take on added abilities. As a result of these abilities, things come to us that we become caretakers of. Things are given into our hands. Some of those are material things. Some of them may be things that are assigned to you even by others—the IRS, your landlord, or the bank. When you sign on the dotted line, things get assigned to your name. That becomes part of the sharing process: extending yourself so that what is assigned to you—what is yours—also goes to others.

Perhaps you have noticed that these blessings are extensions of one another: Loving is an extension of God, caring is an extension of loving, sharing is an extension of caring. As we are more powerfully invoking and expressing our God consciousness, sharing becomes a natural way of being. It is allowing ourselves to be extended.

It's very important to find ways to share. **If you want my prescription for solving the problems on the planet, it is to create conditions and relationships such that everybody feels it's safe to share themselves** and to share their things, situations where I have a trust that if I share with you, you won't violate, abuse, or misuse what I've shared with you.

That may sound like some kind of utopia or heaven: a place where we can openly, honestly share things and it's done the same way in return. That would be a wonderful world. Do you suppose we're going to get that world anytime soon? I don't expect it. So I am practical. I work to have people close to me whom I can openly and honestly share with. And from that base of safety and trust, I can extend my sharing out into the world.

When we are actively loving, caring, and sharing, it leads to the fourth blessing: **health.** John-Roger defines it most beautifully: **"Health is loving who we are.** It's caring for who we are. It's sharing with who we are." It's all of that. That's a healthy vibration, a healthy consciousness, and as we do that, health will come to us.

A while ago, I was with a woman who was basically on her deathbed. She was in a hospital under fairly intense care, and she asked me to come. So I went ready to see somebody who was at death's door, someone who was very dysfunctional physically.

I walked in and found one of the most radiant, alive, vital persons I'd ever met. She was physically alive, not just in the radiation of her being. She did not look or act like a dying person. She was smiling, she was happy, she was joyful, she was grateful, and she was talking about all the blessings in her life.

She was actively involved with and caring for her family and the people who worked in the hospital. Those were her concerns. She was not in any negative way concerned about her health. She was doing what she knew to take care of herself, but there wasn't much she could do about that at this point according to the medical people. The people in the hospital were told, "Her minister is coming by to do a special counseling." So I was being viewed as the guy coming by to do last rites.

I don't do last rites, but what I did was participate in the Spirit with her. It was a great blessing to be part of her process. She taught me a lot, and I'm sure she taught others a great deal about the difference between what is a healthy consciousness, a healthy person, and what happens to the body.

She did die within a week or so. I found it kind of stunning because I was confounded by how she appeared to me and whatever it was that got her physically. So I just decided that God got her. It was not disease that got her. It was her time, and she went with as much power and grace as I've seen. It was really quite magnificent, and it was magnificent to be a part of it.

I learned to distinguish that aspect of health that is a loving consciousness, a caring, sharing consciousness, a vital consciousness. We all have the power to invoke that blessing no matter what condition we find with ourselves.

Wealth is the fifth blessing. We experience the blessing of wealth by participating in the consciousness of wealth. That is a consciousness of being imbued with the power to create. It's important that we set up our attitude that we have been given the power to create wealth. **There is not lack in God's creation.** I say that in loud, bold, clear terms. **There is wealth in God's creation.** Infinite wealth. Unlimited wealth. It comes from the invisible.

If you wonder, "Where is the source of wealth?" it comes from the invisible. Wealth is bringing down what is unmanifest into the manifest. (That is where *all* the blessings come from.) As we invoke that into the material world, it can manifest as anything that money can buy—all of that. But true wealth really is a life of plenty. True wealth is access to the Source that delivers all of our needs. Maybe most importantly, it delivers in the consciousness that we are loved, we are adored, we are served. That's the consciousness of wealth. In a sense, it is recognizing that we are royalty.

Just get the image of royalty in mind. Who is royalty? What kind of places do royal people occupy? Where do they live, and what are their lifestyles like? It doesn't matter how you arrive at that image. You can do past, present, future, fantasy, reality—anything that represents royalty for you.

Then claim that royalty. Recognize that you are royalty. And if you don't know it, then you are a prodigal son or daughter, and you're still wandering, because when you realize who you are, your coming-home party is a celebration that you are royal and that there is nothing that you don't deserve. You deserve it all. That's the consciousness of wealth.

Part of the way this works is in circulation, in distribution, in sharing. **If you want to have greater wealth, you must give, you must share. That's how you create a greater openness to receive.** You demonstrate that you are a good recipient, a good caretaker. You show that when God gives to you, you share the wealth. And that leads to happiness.

To me, **happiness** is just God tickling us. That's my view on it. If you want to know how you become happy, what the secret of happiness is, I'd say, "Get close to God."

Whatever you think getting close to God is, do it. If you don't know where to look, look in your heart. Get close to your heart. Get close to who you are. If necessary, take time to do that, to find out yourself, to maybe shake some of the false images you've adopted.

False images keep us from knowing the truth of who we are. When we attempt to identify with the things that are false, it leads to unhappiness. So if you want to create happiness, identify with what's true and know what's true for you intimately.

We do a lot of self-exploration in my work. You will find many ways in this book to discover yourself. When you do find out aspects of who you are, the truth is to be celebrated—even if it's something you may think is less than wonderful. We are not to judge what we find true about one another or ourselves. We are to love what we find.

If you knew everything about yourself, every single fact, every moment, every event, every occurrence, every thought, every feeling, and then in turn you knew it about everybody else—you would love it all. You would love yourself, and you would love them. You would embrace them and would not turn away. You would not blaspheme them or curse them into hell because if you knew all these things, and you did it to them, you would know you were also doing it to yourself.

Next come **abundance, prosperity,** and **riches.** People ask, "What's the difference between abundance, prosperity, and riches?" Not a lot. But, you know, it's all good stuff.

I include all three together because that relates to having things blessed over and over and over so that you cannot even behold it all, so that it overflows you, and you can't help but share it. Prosperity gets into something that becomes profitable for everyone. It leads to an increase to the extent that the world does become better. That is prosperity. How can it do that? We're invoking what is unmanifest and manifesting it into the world. It actually becomes an increase in the supply, an increase in the blessings, an increase in what's here for us.

17

That's what is happening on the planet. I know we hear a lot about the problems and what's negating the planet. We have a hole in the atmosphere, and we have all these things that have to do with pollution and natural resources. And we have an ever-increasing population. But all those things are really finite.

What I know is that God is the power to solve it all. When we live in that power and live by what that power is, then in our universe, in our world, in the very place where we walk, it is blessed. The air becomes cleaner, the water more pure. There's more for everyone. We go in for the loaves and the fishes, and we look out and somehow there's enough because we do it in that consciousness.

The resources may appear limited, but in the consciousness of "pass this around and keep passing it," the blessings of abundance, prosperity, and riches take place. The planet was created in the consciousness that "there will be enough—there will be more than enough." To me, that is the secret. That's the miracle. When we practice that consciousness, it shall be done.

Now comes the blessing of **touching.** I look at touching as the aspect of connecting. As I see it, it's not enough to be blessed. There's a responsibility that goes with extending the blessing so it goes out—not just to others, but touching the planet and touching the sky and touching inner places.

Sometimes people say, "He's touched in the head. You better stay away from him." The idea is that the person is crazy or they've been cursed or something weird happened to them, and it might be contagious. However, there's also the concept of the divine fool, the one who sees past all the limits and relates to the unlimited power. When we're doing that, we are touching in to the Divine, touching to the one who said (and he wasn't the only one who said it), "Anyone who has seen me has seen the Father,"[1] that one I'm in touch with, in direct contact with, the one who walks on the water, the one who goes through walls, who raises the dead, who finds no barriers, no limits. That's the one we are touching to.

I know if you look in your consciousness, in your heart of hearts, you will find you want to touch God. You want to be face to face with God. Even though you may have fear or doubt about it, if you feel you're not worthy, that you can't do it, that you'll be burnt to a crisp—whatever that negative story line is—I know there's still the part of you that wants to touch God and be touched, to be touched like a child who's picked up, embraced, celebrated, played with, that all the blessings of the kingdom that is your kingdom are bestowed upon you.

I know you hear what's being said here and you hear it in a deep place, because the one who touches me also touches you.

I hope you enjoy this book. I hope you find it more than enjoyable—that you find it useful in assisting you to

1. JOHN 14:9

claim that one inside of you who is to be blessed, who has placed the blessings. Because, truly, the blessings already are.

Baruch Bashan.

A Blessing of Upliftment

☙ DEAR GOD, beloved friend to us all, we ask for your blessing, that we are open to receive and we are open to give.

And we take a moment to let go of our own concerns, that we may find what your concerns are for the highest good.

So we ask that we are lifted, as needed, to see the good in all things and all people. We extend this into whatever has happened. We ask to be fully present here in this place, that we can be glad for whatever is our lot, for all the circumstances in our life.

We may consider situations about our health, our living conditions, the bills we pay, those people in our life we are close to, and especially those who bring us our lessons and anywhere we find misunderstanding, confusion, or hurt.

We open ourselves up now to be ministered unto by the Holy Spirit through the consciousness of the Christ, the one you have anointed to touch to us all, to be an example.

We ask to be an example, that we can demonstrate the ability that is your gift and your blessing, to go forward into this world knowing all is a gift. And when we do not understand, we ask that we are comforted, that we know you enfold us, you embrace us, you walk with us all along the way.

We may need to be shown again and again how to let go, to give up those things that attach us or bind us. Bring in the resonation of the spirit of freedom.

We ask that we can laugh more, smile more, enjoy life more to the fullest extent that can be bestowed, and that we have the wit to live in this way.

Right now, if you can show each one of us what we can do personally to shift ourselves, to make ourselves more available to your purpose, to your will being done, we ask that this be done.

And if a consciousness can be brought forward in whatever way will serve to assist, to hold with us, to remind us of what we are to do in each and every situation, we give thanks for this blessing.

Baruch Bashan.

24

"And God said, 'Let there be light,' and there was light.

God saw that the light was good, and he separated the light from the darkness.

God called the light 'day' and the darkness he called 'night.'

And there was evening, and there was morning—the first day."

GENESIS 1:3–5

Chapter Two

THE BLESSING OF
CHOOSING THE LIGHT

Moment to moment, day in and day out, be open to new experiences by not attaching yourself to the past.

I READ RECENTLY that the word *light* is found in more than one hundred places in the Old Testament of the Bible. I am particularly taken by the reference in the third verse of the first book, Genesis: "Let there be light." Can you imagine God mulling over the Creation and deciding to have light as a major component of life in this world?

If God chose to "let" the light be, was there also a choice present to *not* let there be light? The choice to let there be light is fundamental to our own daily creations. As we encounter this world of shadows and reflections, we have the choice to let the Light of revelation illumine our consciousness to the reality of our experiences.

When you allow yourself to increase your consciousness with the Light, you are also clarifying illusions and protecting yourself from negative input. That probably sounds good to you and, perhaps, even familiar. Then the question is, why aren't you able to maintain the presence of the Light for the highest good?

The simplest answer would be that you are human. **Humans—as much as we might intend otherwise—by our nature turn from the Light. Be grateful that we are always free to choose into the Light.**

Here is an example of a choice I made while traveling on a trans-Atlantic flight with my family, including my then-baby daughter, Claire. A passenger across the aisle became irritated and complained to the flight attendants because Claire had been making "too much noise." (You can probably appreciate that children in their tremendous freedom of expression can also be perceived as a source of irritation.) As the irritation was brought to our attention, I had an opportunity to react negatively or to choose more into the Light.

In my humanity, the negative choices were presented right along with the positive ones. Do I hug the man or challenge him to put up his dukes? With the Light comes the altitude to see every aspect of a situation. I know that peace is present in the absence of againstness. That is very nice, but what do I do when there is againstness present?

In this case, I decided to face it directly. I got up from my seat and walked up to the man in the midst of another round of his complaining to a flight attendant. Once I had his attention, I introduced myself as the father of the baby and asked him what he would like us to do differently. Amazingly, his response was, "Nothing." I told him we had been doing everything we knew to take care of her.

He asked, "Could you make her more quiet?"

"Do you want us to tape her mouth or give her a shot?" I responded.

"No. But when my children fly, they are quiet," was his reply.

I said, "Then you must have perfect children."

"Not by a long shot," was the man's response.

I said, "If you would like us to do something different, please let us know." He thanked me.

By the time I had sat down from my brief talk with the man, Claire was quiet, having been lulled into one of those beautiful slumbers that often would accompany feeding at her mother's breast.

Later, the flight attendant who had taken the most recent complaint thanked me and said that what I did really helped. Then another flight attendant came up to us and stated that she had discussed the situation with the other flight attendants. She related that their point of view was that Claire was really delightful and hadn't been a real problem. They didn't understand why the man was so bothered. She wanted to console us, and she also wanted to console herself, which is understandable. But what about the man?

It would have been easy to move into criticism with the flight attendant, to categorize him negatively for choosing so negatively in relation to my delightful child, who obviously (at least to me) was doing the best she could under the circumstances. However, with the altitude of the Light, I could also see that the man was doing the best he could do under the circumstances. His circumstances were obviously difficult if he found it necessary to be upset with an innocent child who didn't consciously know there was any choice to be quiet.

But what about his innocent child, the one within him? How about sending the Light to lift him and teach him what he needs to learn? The Light was sent to all of us and especially to him.

Later, as I was writing, I could see that the man, too, was quiet while in a beautiful slumber that comes by feeding upon Spirit.

How often have you drawn false conclusions from what was apparent from your perceptions? How often have you reacted strongly to a situation only to later realize you had better choices?

If we took a poll of people who are willing to honestly evaluate their lives, we would likely find that the overwhelming majority are bypassing the better choices. How do you determine the better choices or even the best choice so that you then make it? Spiritually, we can call ourselves forward to the Light for the highest good of all concerned.

It's been said that we teach what we need to learn. It's even more important to demonstrate what we know. We *demonstrate* the Light by first knowing the Light. We can know the Light by experience. With greater experience comes enlightenment.

Wherever you find yourself, you can always choose or ask to have your best intentions revealed. The Light, among other good and wonderful things, does just that. This is all very simple. It can be easy if you will just let the Light radiate through your being and keep your intention on the Light for the highest good of all concerned. And when you forget, you can remind yourself by doing an invocation of the Light in your imagination or by a prayer.

Letting there be Light means being open to what the Light reveals. Right now, open yourself to the Light for the highest good of all concerned. Let go of attachments to the past, to what you think or feel is so, and be open to brand-new experiences of what is present. **Moment to moment, day in and day out, be open to new experiences by not attaching yourself to the past.**

Do you realize that the Light is overflowing with the power to transform all situations to the highest good of all concerned? We all have a full-time occupation to keep ourselves present with the Light so the greatest good and only good can manifest. That means the greatest good is already present and is simply awaiting us to choose back or forward or any way the Light is directed.

Isn't it amazing that each of us always has the choice of the Light for the highest good and nothing but good in every way? "In the beginning, . . . God said, 'Let there be light.'"[1] Let us begin again in the Light now.

Baruch Bashan.

1. GENESIS 1:1–3

A Blessing of Invoking the Light

*Here is a blessing or an invocation that I refer to as
calling in the Light or calling forward the Light. It is
a process that is made sacred more through our intention than any other way. In other words, the form or
the content of the blessing is secondary to our intention
toward the action of "blessing."*

Just now, become more aware of that contact with the
Source of Light inside of you, that yet again we are calling
it forward through the Father-Mother God that is the Source
of Light, that Source which brings forward the highest good
of all concerned.

We ask for the Light first for ourselves, that we clear ourselves
on all levels, surrounding, filling, and protecting ourselves
with this Light. As we hold for this Light, we ask for the

consciousness of the Holy Spirit through God's divine nature to extend this blessing.

We next bless this land. We see this Light anchoring into the very core of the earth. It is a beautiful, radiant Light, illuminating all that is dark, penetrating the densest substances, radiating as a beautiful energy above the land, and blessing all the people and situations on the land.

This Light illuminates the darkness of consciousness anywhere there is pain or disturbance. And especially, Lord, we ask that you go into each consciousness where darkness is stored, hidden by the unconsciousness, that as the darkness was illuminated through your Beloved, once again we make that claim.

We restore the Spirit in each body, regenerating the consciousness of living love, so that each person is blessing himself or herself and all those around, so that each person in their own way awakens to the Light.

We see the places where there is hunger and disturbance being taken care of in their need.

We see a clarifying and purifying of the land, so there is greater and greater beauty and cleanliness in the order of living love.

We, each one of us, hold this consciousness of the Light, anchoring it for all. We offer ourselves once again as servants of the Light, that we are instruments of God's love and acceptance.

We walk in this consciousness wherever we go.

We continuously lift and we are lifted.

We are grateful for this opportunity to be of service. And when we are asked, "Whom do we serve?" we are free in our consciousness to say, "We serve the Lord."

Baruch Bashan.

"There are those who give little
    of the much which they have—
and they give it for recognition
    and their hidden desire
    makes their gifts unwholesome.

And there are those who have little
    and give it all.

These are the believers in life and the bounty of life,
    and their coffer is never empty."

KAHLIL GIBRAN

"He who bends to himself a Joy
Doth the wingèd life destroy;
But he who kisses the Joy as it flies
Lives in Eternity's sunrise."

WILLIAM BLAKE

Chapter Three

THE BLESSING OF
RECEIVING AND GIVING

Soul Transcendence, the direct awareness of our spiritual connection with the Divine, is a process of realizing the detached, nonmaterial state that is the source of our true wealth and prosperity.

WHEN I WAS A YOUNG BOY, I was a very good marbles player. If you are not familiar with marbles, there are a couple of basic games that we played called chasies and pots. In chasies, usually played in a street gutter, players each had one marble to shoot. The object was to hit the other players' marbles on your turn. If you hit the other players' marbles before they hit yours, you won. And vice versa.

In pots, a circle was drawn on a smooth, flat area of bare ground. Each player dropped an agreed-upon number of marbles inside the circle, called the pot. Then, the players would "lag" their "shooter" marble to a line, thus determining the order of play based on whose marble was closest to the lag line.

In turn, each player would place his hand on the line at the edge of the pot to shoot at marbles in the pot. Any marbles that were knocked out of the circle were kept. If a player knocked at least one marble out of the pot and the shooter "stuck" in the pot, then the player got to continue shooting as long as he could keep hitting marbles out while having his shooter stay in the pot, along the lines of a game of billiards.

The basic skills in marbles involve the ability to propel the marble accurately while taking into account the terrain and any boundaries. With pots, there were additional skills in learning how to select the right shooter in size and weight to knock the marbles out of the pot and also make it spin like a top in order to better stay in the pot. Shooters made of marble or agate rock (aggies) were especially revered and hard to come by. The more common marbles were made of glass.

When it came to playing marbles, there was always a basic decision: Are you playing for fun or for keeps? Playing for fun meant that whether you won or lost, you got all your original marbles back when the game was over. Playing for keeps meant that when the game was over, you kept the marbles that you hit or knocked out of the pot. Some players would lose most or all of their marbles. If you didn't have marbles and needed to borrow some to play, you couldn't play for keeps.

In the course of my marble playing, I bought a few marbles and borrowed even fewer. I just about always played for keeps. Once having played for keeps, playing for fun just wasn't as thrilling. If you have played games for money (often referred to as gambling), then you likely know some of the attraction and risk that happen when you play for keeps. As long as you are winning more than losing, the game tends to be enjoyable. This is especially true if whoever is providing your winnings is a good sport or at least neutral.

My winnings at marbles allowed me to build marble fortunes—not just once, but twice—which I stashed in several large coffee cans and shoeboxes. Over time I became so good that besides acquiring hundreds and then thousands of marbles, I found that very few kids wanted to play with me—for obvious reasons. I may be one of the few people around who fully appreciates what it means not only to gain all my marbles but also to lose them all.

My family's move to another city necessitated that I give away my first marble fortune. At least, that's how I remember the situation being presented to me by my father. Despite being pressed to dispose of my marble wealth, I did learn something about the value of being able to share what I have with others. I just gave them all away to a few of my friends (whose number radically increased as the word of my largesse spread through the neighborhood). As an eight-year-old, I learned a lot about the importance of having a great deal of something that others are glad to receive.

The fate of the second fortune of marbles is much more memorable. With the considerable talent I had developed in relation to other players, I soon acquired new cans and boxes full of marbles in our new home. There were so many that I began storing some in our garage so as not to take up too much space in my room, which I shared with my brother.

Gradually, I began to lose any sense of thrill or satisfaction from creating an ever-increasing fortune of marbles. It wasn't just the silent moaning and groaning that usually greeted me when I would appear, ready to play at a game. I got a feeling of what it must be like for bullies to walk up to those they picked on.

One day I just knew the right thing to do was to give all the marbles away. A couple of my buddies really thought I had already "lost my marbles" and urged me to sell them instead. But the more I considered the idea of just plain giving them all away, the more enthused I became. I put the word out that at a certain time one afternoon, anybody who wanted some free marbles should be at the local schoolyard.

I had accumulated so many marbles that I needed a couple of my buddies to help me carry them to the site. The word had obviously gotten out, as plenty of kids of all ages showed up. I had them back up to a distance of about 150 feet away. Yelling, "Keep whatever you find," I began throwing handfuls of marbles. Had I been throwing diamonds, gems, and gold coins, I hardly think the response could have been any more intense. All these kids were madly scurrying after each and every marble.

Within seconds of the first throws, observing the excited and joyful responses, I could hardly remain standing as fits of laughter overcame me. **There was an amazing sense of delight in freely and with abandon giving away the very things I had so intensely sought to acquire and possess for so long.** It was an enormous source of laughter to see others so intently focusing on acquiring the very things I was dispossessing myself of with great relish.

Perhaps you can appreciate, as I do, the part of St. Francis' life in which he is reputed to have gone to a tower in the home of his prosperous merchant father to throw very valuable garments and bolts of cloth to excitedly happy people on the street below, much to his father's horror. This incident occurred at the time of St. Francis' spiritual emancipation and led to his dedication to live by the means of his Father in Spirit rather than the considerable means and inheritance of his physical father.

It is not too soon to consider that one day you will, as will everyone, be giving up everything you possess in this world. Do you realize that you will have the same opportunity to delight in dispossessing yourself of the materiality of this world? Would you rather make your passing a futile effort to hang on, not letting go in the slightest way? Or will you already be detached and freely letting go of all that you possess and have acquired?

Soul Transcendence, the direct awareness of our spiritual connection with the Divine, is a process of realizing the detached, nonmaterial state that is the source of our true wealth and prosperity. It is high time to practice expanding our abundance and riches as we learn to let it all go and pass it on to those who are able to receive.

Many sacred scriptures tell us that the Lord gives and the Lord takes away. It is not too smart to attach

ourselves to the materiality of this world such that when the Lord gives or takes away, we are ill-prepared for either. It is our heritage to learn to freely receive and give. This is a great key to a life of ever-increasing abundance and riches. The source of the supply is unlimited, and the opportunities on the planet are more plentiful than ever.

There is always more than enough for everyone to keep playing. The Lord's game is played for fun and for keeps. Share your wealth, that the unlimited Divine Source may replenish you evermore.

Baruch Bashan.

A Blessing of Liberation

❧ LORD, we do ask for your blessing, extending through us as a gift.

As those who extend in your purpose to express your blessings, we ask that you visit each of us personally at this time, to work with us in our relationship to this world.

We ask that you bring your great Light that is the Holy Spirit, through the one we know as Lord of us all, to sit down with us, to visit us where we live, to look in every corner, every aspect of what we have created.

We ask this through all that has been created, that we have a balancing here and now, a lifting of what is no longer necessary, and a placement of your grace.

We claim the debts are paid, through this action of your Beloved that comes in and sits with us now, that we are the

Beloved, and we do partake of these blessings, the lifting of the debt.

We claim the healing, the balancing for ourselves, for those we have entangled through unnecessary actions.

And now we claim that you are liberating us again and straightening our consciousness, so that we live according to what is true, what is your love and is unconditional to all. We set this purpose supreme, carrying it in our hearts, sanctifying our dedication, acting upon our devotion anew, putting aside our attachments and our distractions, bringing us to our wisdom that we will act true to our divine nature, that we will find the direct way you have placed before us, the clarity, the strength, and the knowledge.

We give thanks that you fill our hearts, that we affirm with our breath in each moment. We breathe in the blessings. We breathe out our gifts, our sacrifice, willingly, openly, and freely unto all. Increase us evermore, that we may expand past all limitation, finding ourselves transcending and knowing ourselves in the Soul.

We accept your patience, the patience that always endures and overcomes.

We accept your peace, the peace that is the understanding that it is done.

Baruch Bashan.

47

"Love, now a universal birth,
From heart to heart is stealing:
From earth to man, from man to earth: It is the hour of
  feeling.
One moment now may give us more
  than years of toiling reason;
And from the blessed power that rolls about, below,
  above
We'll frame the measure of our souls: They shall be
  tuned to love."

WILLIAM WORDSWORTH

"If you seek to soar to heaven,
make friends with all men.
Never harbor a grudge in your heart.
The joy of friendship is Paradise.
When you talk of enemies,
thorns and snakes fill your heart."

RUMI

Chapter Four

THE BLESSING OF

LOVING ONE ANOTHER

God always answers our call. The question is, are we listening?

I RECEIVED A LETTER from a dear friend in 1992, which dealt with the situation brought to the world's attention as a result of the rioting in Los Angeles after the verdict in the Rodney King trial. He wrote in part,

I was pretty upset by the L.A. riots. Several days have passed and I am starting to get some altitude on the situation, but I could use some assistance in gaining greater clarity.

Today when a memo was sent around my office for food donations for South Central Los Angeles residents, I immediately passed the word to my fellow employees. I was surprised at the response, which generally boiled down to: "Why should we help people who burned down their own neighborhood?" I spoke as convincingly as I could in favor of assisting those in need, but my words seemed to have no impact, given the emotional energy my friends had on the topic.

When I got home, I shared the experience with my wife and heard that my daughter had been throwing up during the day. My wife and I considered what was affecting my daughter, and one of the things we came up with was that she was being affected by negativity coming from many levels. It struck me that this whole situation was another challenge to choose into the Light.

I reflected on all the things I had heard on the radio that day about people mobilizing to provide aid to the South Central residents. I realized that a strong statement of unconditional loving and forgiveness could be communicated by offering assistance not only to "innocent victims" but also to anyone who requested it.

As I focused on the power of those actions, I wondered if the riots came about to offer us a unique opportunity to cross the self-imposed borders that exist between neighborhoods and create a sense that each of us is ultimately responsible for the quality of life in this area that has been named "the City of Angels." I'd be grateful to hear your thoughts and feedback.

This was my response to his letter:

It will always be true that each situation in our lives is a challenge and an opportunity to choose into the Light. The only difference is the degree to which we find ourselves challenged by the nature of each situation. Perhaps it is most challenging to choose into the Light when we are happy and contented because we have a tendency to forget the importance of choosing the Light when we are at our best.

There is a wartime saying: "Everybody in a foxhole knows God." When we are at our worst, even the most devout unbelievers call upon God. **God always answers our call. The question is, are we listening?** Are we hearing God's answers and abiding by those answers?

Perhaps the obvious answer to that question is no, considering the L.A. riots and any number of other situations in the world where there is violence, disease, corruption, injustice, and the like. Humans have been consistently ignoring and violating the answer from God from time immemorial. The result is the mess in which we individually and collectively find ourselves in the world today.

One of the great answers that applies to all of us is to "love your enemies."[1] You might pose this idea to your colleagues to find out how they would respond. Surely the path to loving your enemies is entered by forgiveness and traversed by an unconditional willingness to let go of the past and live in the presence of loving.

We must learn to break down the barriers of separation caused by patterns of hatred and bigotry that have been repeated across generations and cultures. The real

53

1. MATTHEW 5:44

"enemy" is what lives inside of us as hatred, fear, condemnation, indifference, etc. We shall overcome the enemies that we encounter inside or outside with unconditional loving and acceptance. We demonstrate the loving by the choices we make and where we place our focus. During times of powerful upheaval and negativity raging in the world, we often question our ability to overcome—or even survive—the enemies that confront us.

The answer is always to stop the cycles of perpetual negativity both individually and collectively by fulfilling the call to love unconditionally. Revenge has always been justified by vengeance, hatred by hatred, and violence by violence. Loving is justified by loving, caring by caring, and giving by giving. **The cycle of God, the good, is broken by a single act of negativity. The cycle of negativity is stopped by choosing the good—not just once, but again and again until it is goodness that prevails in your life and in our world altogether.**

One day each of us will understand that negativity, while being a choice, is never God's answer or God's intention for anyone, no matter how evil they have chosen to be. God's business is always unconditional loving and forgiveness of all—which still includes responsibility and stopping the againstness that confronts us.

Many have said that much of the disturbance and upheaval in the world is due to the differences between the "haves" and the "have-nots." There is no such thing. Either we all have or we all have not. It is along the lines of the famous quote from Shakespeare: "To be or not to be."

There are great diversities in the environmental and cultural conditions in which people live throughout the world. These conditions range from the most wonderful to the most despicable. Regardless, **God has an answer that supersedes every condition extending through all of his creation. The answer, now and forevermore, is to love.** Love is what we all have always. The have-not is when we—any one of us at any moment—deny love to ourselves or others or any thing.

It takes great strength to see the face of God in those who are acting with destruction as their expression. Each and every time we are confronted by negativity in others and the situations we face, we must strive toward God's answer to all of the creation: "love one another, as I have loved you,"[2] "love your neighbor as yourself,"[3] and love all of creation with "all thy heart, and with all thy soul, and with all thy mind."[4]

Be glad that you have been shaken, and know that the shaking serves you and all who are affected to find the truth that is solid. Be glad that you have any opportunity, great or small, to express your charity and compassion regardless of the resistance or indifference you may face. Loving is your true nature, as well as the true nature of all those who act against it by choosing negativity. This, in part, is God's calling unto each of us. This, in part, is the

2. JOHN 15:12
3. MATTHEW 19:19
4. MATTHEW 22:37

divine action and the partaking in the blessings that already are.

Perhaps you can take a cue from Tom Sawyer, whose fence needed painting on a day of leisure. Present the situation of helping the people of South Central Los Angeles, a task of caring for our brother in his time of need, as a light and fun-filled process that all will want to join in. You might ask your colleagues what they suppose might happen to them if they lived in the conditions of South Central Los Angeles day in and day out with matters seemingly becoming only worse and worse.

When we learn to consider the pain and upset that a person must carry within them in order to act negatively, we then come to a compassionate understanding that we would not want to do anything to inflict more hurt upon them. We, in fact, realize that to bring harm upon another is to bring harm upon ourselves. We simply refuse a response of anything less than loving. We rejoice in the upliftment of our brother or sister as much as we would rejoice in the upliftment of ourselves. When two or more of us are rejoicing in one another's upliftment, we shall each see God's face rejoicing with us.

Baruch Bashan.

A Blessing of Surrender

☙ DEAR LORD, let us be awakened now, again.
Let us put aside our mind that tells us that you are not here
and now. Let us put aside our doubts and our fears.

Lift us to the heart of the Spirit. Reveal again our joy, the
celebration of our life as a Soul, as one who came into this
world full of goodness, full of purity and dedication to
truth, and alive with unceasing love through overflowing
abundance, prosperity, and goodness for all.

Let us become a clear example of God's life in this world.
Quicken that Spirit in us. Cast away those things that keep
us in unknowing so that we become knowers of God.

Let us have a vision now, an experience within that we take
into this world, where we see our feet firmly upon the
ground, that we welcome this day. We welcome the
circumstances in which we find ourselves. We see the beauty,

we know the harmony and the peace that is your will being done.

Let us be bold and clear in our expression of the Spirit. There's no need to hold back here. Our goodness is full. It is strong. Let us behold you by your Spirit. The world can contain it no more. It directs us into our liberation; it lifts us beyond the limitations we find here.

We are not downtrodden by what we see in the world. We are not deterred by the pessimism, the negativity, the debts, the lack, or the hatred we may encounter in ourselves or others. We are not downtrodden by anything, as we are raised up by every situation.

We lift ourselves in your consciousness and in your energy. We are straightened wherever we have been bent by the weight of judgments or shame. In whatever ways we have been hardened and encased in ritualized ideas and concepts of restriction, we cast them away freely.

We reflect upon that which is the heart and the love and the joy, expanding past any limitations, any chains that would imprison our oneness with you.

We forgive ourselves for looking upon ourselves and others as prisoners, as less than divine. This is not our consciousness of love.

We bless ourselves as we bless one another.

We restore this world to a garden, to a pristine world, where good flourishes and harmony and peace are all that can be seen.

We are your children, bringing your deeds home. We gladly accept the opening of our heart that reveals your truth. Quicken us once again. Raise our vibration; lift us in your purpose. We are open. We are complete in our oneness with you.

We sing your praise. We hear your melody. The Sound and Light are all around.

Sweet surrender again. We let go. We let you, God.

Baruch Bashan.

A Blessing of the Holy Presence

❧ FATHER-MOTHER GOD, we ask to know your presence
     inside of us now,
that we become more conscious of your Light and your love
     surrounding, filling, and protecting each one of us,
that we call ourselves forward, active in your purpose.

We ask for your alignment, that we are open to change.
We are open to letting go of what no longer serves.
We ask for the direction, the strength, the willingness
     so that we choose to move upon the highest good of all
          concerned,
that with each breath we are activating this consciousness
that serves,
     that knows the Christ, that one who is anointed by you,
     preparing the way, awakening the spirit within,
that this is the Holy Spirit we breathe.

This is the Holy Spirit that awakens us now,
    a consciousness of your breath,
that your thoughts, your emotions are what move us,
    are what we ask for and surrender to
    as a process of the Divine each moment.

We ask that you bring to mind whatever it is we need to
    learn.
We ask to be conscious to know what would serve us to let
    go of,
    that we let you take hold,
    that we can become one with you as your will is done.

Bless all the small things.
Bless the things that we live with,
    the conditions that we were born with—
    bless it all.

We ask this blessing to extend out into the world
    and into all the forces and consciousness
    that influence this world through time.
We are those calling forth the greatest blessings.
Whatever part we are to play, we offer ourselves willingly as a
    dedication.

And we know the simplicity of this movement
is to love one another as you have loved us,
that we take heart in you.

Baruch Bashan.

"It is necessary to keep in mind that perfection
is not achieved on the physical level:
With the physical body, no one is perfect.

In Soul expression, you are already perfect;
Everyone is.

In the consciousness of the body, emotions, and mind,
you are working to bring yourself into balance
so you can more readily see the Soul's perfection."

JOHN-ROGER

Chapter Five

THE BLESSING OF
ACCEPTING THE PERFECTION

The best choices will always be the most loving.

WHEN I WAS YOUNG I often heard the expressions, "Behave yourself," and "Be on your best behavior." While I have always managed to behave myself one way or another, I have not always been on my best behavior. Like many of us, there is a part of me that's hoping that one of these days I am going to get it right once and for all.

At first, behaving myself meant primarily staying out of trouble with my parents, brother, sister, babysitters, teachers, bullies, teasers, and the like. I was often less than successful. Life was a series of episodes in which trouble was always on the horizon. No matter what I did, I could not stay out of trouble.

You might wonder just what kind of trouble I mean. I have not been imprisoned. I have not been hospitalized except when I was quarantined with a severe case of the measles. I was not abused by any standard of society. I never went hungry or lacked for clothing or shelter. I was generally liked by my family and peers and was afforded a lot of education and opportunities. I grew up in one of the most prosperous cultures in the world. By most standards, I would be considered to have had a very fortunate life right up to this moment. So what was my trouble?

Nothing, as in "no-thing." The problem was actually my perception that there was trouble or a problem. Whenever I interpreted a situation to be troublesome or problematic, then it was. And conversely, when I decided that the situation was not a problem, then it was not.

Perhaps you have heard the admonishment, "Judge not, that ye be not judged."[1] In other words, do not judge unless you want to become that judgment. Some people might question this, asking, "Are you saying that if I break my leg and it really hurts, then I should pretend my leg is not broken and does not hurt?" No, I am not suggesting you deny your experience. In fact, it is imperative to acknowledge your experience.

What I am saying is that **a judgment is a negative and unnecessary interpretation of your experience.** If you decide that because your leg is broken and hurts, your life is ruined, you have judged yourself and your situation. Likewise, if you declare your life not worth living and in turn curse your existence, you have again judged yourself.

Judgments can also be projected toward other people and things outside of yourself. If you pick up the newspapers and read about people or events that you then decide are bad, evil, wrong, etc., then you have judged and set

1. MATTHEW 7:1

yourself up to become the nature of your judgments. Some people might ask, "But what about all the terrible things that people do and that happen in the world? Am I supposed to pretend they are wonderful and that there are not any problems and troubles in the world?" No. Judging takes place when you unnecessarily and negatively interpret what you experience or perceive.

I look upon negativity and pain as messengers of better opportunities that are available. Negativity and pain tell us that things could be better and that, often, the way things are is unnecessary or available for improvement. Some people might ask, "What about situations when the negativity and pain get worse and worse no matter what I do?" I have often heard John-Roger refer to his mother's saying, "If it does not kill you, it will strengthen you." And what if it does kill you? **In reality, only the body dies. *You* live on, strengthened by all of your experiences, no matter how severe.**

Am I saying that none of the occurrences, situations, pain, negativity, and the like in the world is a problem? That is exactly what I am saying when problems are represented as tragedy, againstness, discouragement, and so on. A world without problems is a perfect world. **God's world is a perfect world. It is not without trials and lessons, but it is only our human judgments that create the illusion that God's world—the world we are living in—is imperfect.**

One day when I was twenty years old and about to graduate from college, the Spirit very powerfully impressed upon me this message: "Life is what you make it." I realized that I could choose exactly what I make my life. I was ecstatic with this revelation.

On the same day, my girlfriend at that time had planned a lunch during which I was to meet her father, who was passing through our vicinity on a business trip. It was to be our first meeting, and she had her heart set on it.

In the midst of my ecstatic revelation, she called me. She was very upset because her father had to cancel the lunch. I, however, was still in the ecstatic revelation of how my life was what I make it. I saw how this change of events was perfect, and I told her so. She was not thrilled to hear this from me, and it, of course, made her more upset. I attempted to explain to her that we could still have a great day—even a better day—since the lunch was canceled. She became increasingly more upset and confused. I went on, trying to explain that I would love to meet her father but that we could make the day as wonderful as we wanted no matter what was going on. More confusion.

In that moment, I realized that if I was going to love her in a way she could understand, then I would have to move out of the consciousness of ecstasy. She thought I was crazy or that something was terribly wrong with me. I chose to return to my usual serious, rigid expression so that she would relate to me more as the person she had known instead of continuing to express the real beingness I had found inside.

I had a profound experience that day of the challenges involved in expressing the nature of the Soul in a world that is powerfully identified with problems and neg-ativity. **Only by connecting with the nature of the Spirit can we realize that all the problems and negativity in the world are just situations in which we decide what we want to make of them.** All things considered, why not make the best choices we can and use everything for our upliftment and learning?

The best choices will always be the most loving. No matter what confronts you inwardly or outwardly, look for the most loving choices and direct your expression into actions that reflect those choices. There is no limit to the power of loving. Loving is supreme in this world and in the worlds to come. You will be on your best behavior when you make your life loving every day and in every way. We are here to become the embodiment of loving.

Baruch Bashan.

A Blessing of Truth and Love

This is a blessing for preparing a place in each and every moment, so we really are prepared for what comes forth. It's important to know that what comes forth first is from within and, also, that the nature of our consciousness in this world is that it, too, is coming outside of us, so that we get to experience God's creation through many, many dimensions.

How do we, then, prepare for the experiences coming forward from within and all around? We prepare by letting go, trusting in God's will being done, and calling ourselves forward in this moment in love and Light, that that is all we are. And anything less than love and Light we release and know that it is truly nothing. It comes from nothing, it goes to nothing, and what remains is true love—the love that is true, the truth that is love.

WE OPEN OURSELVES just now to have that experience of love and truth in all things. In whatever we experience or encounter, whether it is something we like or do not like, whether it is expected or unexpected, regardless of the nature, we embrace all in truth and love by letting go and trusting in God's will.

This will is all-encompassing, in your breath—breathing in and breathing out. And just as you can experience your breath as a constant process, in and out, so, too, experience your love as a constant process, in and out.

We also call forward a higher consciousness now, to reveal to us what we are to do. And what we are to do, we accept as a process that is done instantly in each moment, through unconditional acceptance, through cooperation, knowing that all things come in some way that serves, all things lift, all things are a source of learning and growth in the very best way. So whatever you consider right now, you see in truth, being revealed in Light, revealed in love.

Find your courage, the consciousness that comes through strength, the strength that is the purpose of God, the intention of God's will being done.

God's will takes place through a state of perfection. In this perfection, nothing needs to change and everything is changing. And so you always have an opportunity to let go, to allow for the change that is God's will, to release your will that comes through any state of illusion and falsehood, and to accept completely all that is your experience, the very truth of who you are, the truth in all things.

In this moment you have an opportunity to once again release through time, through past actions, that in the Light, in the love that is the Christ, the Holy Spirit, you are being lifted. You are being clarified, purified, and cleansed. You are being renewed into the Holy of Holies, the pure state of your Soul, the consciousness of God.

And from this day forward, and in this moment, you are to honor the Beloved, upholding the sacredness, the joy, that the consciousness of grace is the consciousness of forgiveness. So forgive. And smile upon your creation as you smile upon all of God's creation.

Baruch Bashan.

"*If you would learn the secret of Soul Transcendence,
look only for the good,
for the Divine in people and things,
And all the rest leave to God.*"

JOHN-ROGER

"*Accustom yourself
always to look to Divinity.*"

PYTHAGORAS

Chapter Six

THE BLESSING OF SEEING
THE GOOD IN ALL THINGS

Be careful what you ask for because it leads to
what you seek, which leads to what you find.

I CARRY AROUND A LITTLE CARD with a quote that reads, "If you would learn the secret of Soul Transcendence, look only for the good, for the Divine in people and things, and All the rest leave to God." I carry it around with me because, at times, I need to be reminded. I have had moments of difficulty seeing the good—not only in people but also in events, in feelings, in thoughts, and in various situations.

If I consider myself a Soul (which I do), then I cannot get away from that statement as a standard for living. It is as if I am being told, "Solve this and the door is open, and you are going to make it through this world as a Soul." For me to work this principle, **I need to look at each challenging person, situation, or thing and tell myself, "There has got to be some good in there somewhere. There is always good. The Divine is always present." My job is to continuously look for the good and the Divine.**

This is aligned with Bible scripture: "Seek ye first the kingdom of God, and his righteousness; and all these things shall be added unto you."[1] *Looking* and *seeking* are words that are closely related. Seeking or looking does not mean we must first know, understand, or believe. It does necessitate having something to look for. So if I will just look for the good and the Divine—and trust it is there—that is the secret.

Sometimes I have attempted to curse the invisible, God, because I have convinced myself that looking for the good will not work. I have thought, "This is a situation that is evil. This is a person who has been bad. There is no way that I am going to find good here." I saw things as wrong or bad. I was saying, "It is not me that is wrong or bad. It is that." In the process, I was making what appeared as wrong or bad something apart from me.

Herein lies a major key, because **regardless of how bad or wrong I perceive something, I still have an opportunity to look for the good in the midst of my "bad" experience.** It seems as if on the one side, I hear this little voice quietly saying, "If you will see the good, if you will see the Divine, . . ." and on the other side, a voice saying, "No, I do not want to look for that." I am actually wrestling with the good by not wanting to look. When I do look, the good, the Divine, always appears to me. Then I conclude, "You are right." I realize how silly I am being to stop whenever I see the bad, when I could instead be looking and finding the good.

1. MATTHEW 6:33

This realization often is accompanied by feelings of embarrassment and amusement. I have to admit how bad, wrong, or foolish I was to judge. Then I may have my self-judgment to deal with. But at least I have gotten my focus back with me. It is much easier to deal with that way.

Attempting to place the problem outside of me and blaming others is futile. When I bring the responsibility back with me, things are easier to manage because I am starting to take authority over the situation.

Looking for the good does not necessarily feel good. I have asked myself, "How do I let go of this judgment now that I am dealing with myself? I am the one who is all these negative things I was recognizing. It was never their fault."

That can be a tough one to look at. When I remember the Christian saying, "Inasmuch as ye have done it to one of the least of these my brethren, ye have done it unto me,"[2] that is when I hang my head. I cannot say, "Oh, well, not you, Lord. I did not do that to you." My realization is, "Yes, I did do it to you when I did it to the least of them."

Does referring to "the least of them" include only people? Maybe it is also the least thing. What if the reality is that when you kick your bumper or the door of your car, you did it to the Lord? One day that hit me, and I thought, "Oh, my God, how am I ever going to be cleared of all my transgressions?" That was the day I really began

2. MATTHEW 25:40

to know forgiveness. I began to know that when I look for the good and for the Divine, then good and the Divine will be added unto me.

That is the key to a really great relationship—to see the good in all the things I am dealing with. Seeing the good really keeps me aligned inside. When I am aligned, everything is just fine. Those are the days I am singing and dancing in peace and loving. I know that when I am not, I have lost track. Somehow I lost track of the good, and my seeking has become something less than the Divine. This actually turns out to be good if I am smart enough to real-ize that **in order to know that I have lost track of the Divine, part of me must also know where the Divine is.**

I can always begin the process of getting back on track with the Divine by forgiving myself for forgetting that good is in all things. For me, this is part of the process of letting go and letting God, for my trust is that *all* things come out of God—and whatever comes out of God is good!

The process of moving into the Divine involves each one of us. We begin moving more into the Divine each time we look for the good and seek the Divine. The divine process is simply looking and seeking toward the highest good. The challenging part of the process is maintaining that focus. It is always worth meeting that challenge. Besides, there is no way out of the good, as that is always present. You can find it laughing; you can find it crying. You can find it kicking; you can find it screaming. However we see people and things, as we claim the blessings present, then we are going to find the good because that is always present.

Regardless of what has happened or whether we understand, we can open ourselves to God's protection and grace. I am still learning how to do that. I am still humble. I do not pretend that I have control over it. I am seeking. I know where my intention is, and that is to go to God. That is the way I put it inside of myself. I do not necessarily care if anybody else understands what that means because that is between God and me.

When I start owning that relationship with God, it becomes a oneness. I start owning that when I do it to "the least of them," I did it to me. And when I do it to "the greatest one," I also did it to me. It is all me, and there is no part of the relationship that is not me.

I understand that there is a relative nature to this, an individual nature for everyone to experience for themselves. My attitude is that I am given this body, and God says, "That is yours to manage. I will take care of the rest." I think that is a wonderful relationship—that God takes care of the rest and makes it really clear to me what is mine.

While I am in this world, I always take my body with me. I understand that my body goes with this world, so I take care of it. My attitude is that the body is a temple. This is a place where God can dwell. What am I doing to make it a place where God is welcome?

Make a place for the Divine to dwell with you. It already does. You can allow yourself to harmonize more with the Divine, so that the Divine fully becomes you. Be the Divine in your words, in your actions, and in your thoughts. When you become one with the highest consciousness, which is God, there is nothing that cannot be overcome because that is the one who overcomes all things, who overcomes the world. When you are dealing with things that get in the way of the Divine, you are dealing with the lower consciousness. You are dealing with the lie, the deceit, or the illusion. The question becomes, "Whom do you serve? Whom do you follow?" The Bible puts it this way: "Choose you this day whom ye will serve."[3]

I realized that it comes down to a moment-to-moment choice to serve the highest good. It is not enough for me to do it once today and figure that is it. I have to keep choosing. I want to do it with every breath. I find out when I am not choosing the highest good because I start getting into negativity. Negativity starts showing up in my face and in my clothes and in my car. It is like it is everywhere. I turn on the TV and it is there. When I am in that place, I think I cannot get away from it. But then comes the quiet voice: "Yes, you can. When you go to the consciousness that overcomes negativity, you can see the good in all things." Then what appears to be bad is transformed by the good things being added unto me.

The highest consciousness sees the good in all things. That is its nature. When you are not seeing things that

3. Joshua 24:15

way, move. Shift your focus. Seek the good, and surely the good and, even more, the highest good that is the Divine will be added unto you until you know the blessings are present.

You might ask, "Where do I go?" Go to God. "Who is God?" God is love. Start there. Right where you are, ask, "How can I love this person and this situation?"

Ask. That is a key to seeking. Seeking is a key to finding. **Be careful what you ask for because it leads to what you seek, which leads to what you find.**

When something is in your way, ask yourself how you can love it. That is when you will find out just how willing you are to seek the good and the Divine. Once you find the good and the Divine in all things, then you will know that you are always blessed. The blessings dwell with you. The blessings find you because you seek them, knowing they are always with you.

Baruch Bashan.

A Blessing of Renewal

🙠 LET US PRAY.

Lord God, we ask that you visit each one of us intimately now, so that we can know you personally, that if we have placed any barriers and separation through our misdeeds, through our misunderstanding, through our forgetfulness, we ask that this be lifted at this time, that we embrace you fully and completely, that there is nothing that we would hide, that as you embrace us, we are cleansed, we are renewed and restored to the glory of God, by which we were made.

And we ask for your spark that is the Divine to be ignited, so that we are a new Light, a new consciousness that sees the good in all things, and that as you have bestowed the spark of the Divine on us once again, so that we are a new Light, we carry forth a dedication to serve, that we go forth in the Light that is the loving consciousness toward all.

We give thanks for this grace, the mercy that you extend to us, through your forgiveness.

We give thanks for your constant understanding of what we have done, that you never hold even one thing against us. It is not your nature. And we ask that we, too, acknowledge this nature of unconditional loving.

We choose this moment in your blessing that you place in our heart and in our radiant being. We look upon this world in this mercy, this consciousness of the Beloved, your Anointed, that we do accept this anointing at this time.

By your grace, we initiate the advent of our anointing, that we are born again in the Divine, renewed in the Divine, that we walk as your Beloved, taking joy in the silence of your being. And through compassionate eyes and in our own unique ways, we do extend your caring.

And we would ask to be known as your friends.

Baruch Bashan.

A Blessing of Sanctification

❧ LORD GOD, dearly Beloved, as your children gathered
   here before you,

we ask that you bless us with your loving embrace—

that each one of us can know right now that we are your
   children,

that you embrace us in love and caring,

that we are cherished,

and that you forgive us for our errors, for what we do not
   know or do not understand,

that in this consciousness of the Christ,

the negativity, the burdens of this world are all lifted and
   cleared away,

that we can come and abide with you,

that you have a place prepared for us—a place of beauty,
   a place of sacredness that is sanctified and of your
   holy nature,

that we breathe in this holy nature, and we breathe it out.

We ask you to straighten us as you see fit,

that we trust and let go of our fears.

We let go of our ways that move us astray, move us into
   darkness and pain.

We ask to awaken to the Spirit of the Divine, the Holy Spirit,

that we are comforted once again, knowing your will is
   being done,

that we are grateful for our life, such as it is,

for this world, such as it is.

We are not here to fight or to struggle.

We are here to love and to be loved.

And let us hear that still, clear voice of direction,

the voice of truth,

living in and abiding in us each day,

that we are guided into ever greater blessings.

Baruch Bashan.

"Swiftly arose and spread around me the peace and
    knowledge that pass all the argument of the earth,
And I know that the hand of God is the promise of my
    own,
And I know that the spirit of God is the brother of my
    own,
And that all the men ever born are also my brothers, and
    the women my sisters and lovers,
And that a kelson of the creation is love..."

WALT WHITMAN

"Soul, whose organ he is,
would he let it appear through his actions,
would make our knees bend.
When it breathes through his intellect, it is genius;
when it breathes through his will it is virtue;
when it ploughs through his affection,
it is love."

RALPH WALDO EMERSON

Chapter Seven

THE BLESSING OF
ALIGNING WITH GOD

*The inner reality of Spirit will always be better
than the outer manifestation.*

To DO GOD'S WORK is to be spiritually directed, which translates to being inner-directed. Those who are inner-directed by the Spirit will outwardly attempt to cooperate and come into the flow of the manifestation of Spirit. This attempt is often wrought with awkwardness, difficulty, arduousness, and the sandpapering of personalities.

The inner reality of Spirit will always be better than the outer manifestation. Spirit is the source of inspiration within you. The place of inspiration is always more pristine, more clear, more bright, more wonderful than what ends up showing outwardly. When you partake in outer loving and outer blessings, it really is a time to praise and to be thankful that the *inner* blessing could also take place *outside* of you.

The blessings that already are can be reflected outside of you. The connection between the inner and the outer blessings is loving. **The common language of the Spirit on this level is loving.** Always and forever, firstly and lastly, make sure that whatever you do is done through loving.

Representing the Spirit into the world is a great responsibility as well as a great opportunity because Spirit is always readily available to those who would choose back. **By just looking to align with Spirit, you automatically enter a process of releasing yourself from your lower nature and all its attendant illusions and negativity.**

Those who are choosing to serve the Spirit are committing to move into alignment and to maintain that alignment. You will be challenged by your lower nature as soon as you make the commitment to align with Spirit, which is your higher nature. Your lower nature will drive you toward accomplishing things and attaining recognition in the world. Your higher nature will direct you into and through experiences that enlighten and nurture your being by utilizing everything that you do or that happens to you in the world as a means of learning and growing.

Everyone has the capacity to know what is working by the wisdom that comes through experience. You will know what is working by the presence of the Spirit. The presence of Spirit comes by way of loving, joy, laughter, peace, and the ease by which you can accept and cooperate with your movement of spiritual inner awareness moment to moment. Right now, for example.

We are all, on this level, subject to being tested by the negative power in our spiritual knowing. For those working in Spirit, the loyalty is to the Soul—the God aspect of your being. The only "other" that you are in relationship with is God. As you come into the experience and communion with God, you find out, "Oh, I am God and God is who I am."

You can take greater advantage of this communion with God. Always move from the information into the experience of God as directly as you can. Always strive to be in the place inside of you where you partake in the Spirit.

Have the experience right now that you are breathing in the Spirit. Your breath is God's breath. As you breathe out, the purity, the holiness, the loving that is God breathes out. You become the Holy Breath as you live your life in this world.

This place inside of you is a place of silence, a place of utmost simplicity, as you breathe in and out with God. Know that you are always doing this breathing with God, and God is breathing with you. Open your conscious awareness for greater knowing of God than ever before. Experience the ease of God's breath in you, the ease that is actually around you in the world, even with all the complications and difficulties. With whatever pain and struggle that are present in the world now or are yet to come, God's breath is always easy.

The breath of God brings life and the loving that you are. It brings the presence of God through all ages, through all time. This breath initiates the healing, the reawakening, and the realization of who you are in the Divine. It is the emanation that awakens all.

You are in this Holy Breath of God. In each moment, renew your faith. Renew your faith in *this* moment. Take this moment to rededicate yourself to God's love and doing God's will through you into this world and into all your choices into the worlds to come. You are renewing your holy sacrament to become one with God. God smiles upon you and welcomes your being. You are embraced in God's love.

Baruch Bashan.

A Blessing of
Alignment with God

*Take in a deep breath, and as you breathe out, you can
let go of any physical tension or discomfort, coming
into a greater ease on all levels. Take in another deep
breath, and this time as you breathe out, let go of any
emotional burdens, fears, or anxieties.*

*Breathe in deeply again, and as you breathe out, you
may release any mental preoccupations or distractions.
You can let go of anything that would prevent you
from being right here now. You are in complete
harmony and balance with your entire experience.*

*You find you are using this process as a means to take
care of yourself and to direct yourself in a way that
will support you in your upliftment and unfoldment.
You are aware of the perfect protection of God enfold-*

ing you completely. Now your breathing can move into an easy and natural rhythm. You can allow the loving and peace of who you are to flow in and out of you with each breath. Now you call yourself forward into the Light.

&ℰ FATHER-MOTHER GOD, we ask right now for the presence of the Light of the Holy Spirit and the Christ to surround, fill, and protect each one of us, so that whatever takes place during this process will be for the highest good of all concerned.

We also ask that the Christ Consciousness work with us and accompany us on this journey, to assist us in moving beyond any judgments, fears, or limitations that we may have imposed on ourselves or others or that we have accepted from others as an imposition upon ourselves up until now.

And for anything that is taken from us at this time, we ask that something of equal or greater value be put in its place.

We would also ask for a special blessing that through this process of aligning ourselves with the highest good, we may open to a new awareness of our divinity and our greatest trusting of God's love for us.

We now find our willingness to receive a deeper experience of the unconditional love of God. And may we surrender completely to the grace, fulfillment, and wisdom of God that is available to each of us in every moment of our lives.

We claim our heritage to forever dwell in the heart of God.

Now we fully align and atone with the Holy Spirit. Lord, we are grateful for all the blessings that you have placed upon us and that we are about to receive as we fully realize that thy will is done.

And so it is.

Baruch Bashan.

"*I haven't even begun to get with God completely,*
but as soon as I move toward God inside of me
   and start viewing what is taking place,
I start realizing that whatever is taking place,
whatever is present,
is just fine.
I realize that I'll get through it;
I'll survive it.
I start seeing that whatever is going on
   is not going to last,
that things change,
and that everything is in motion.
Then, as I go a little bit higher in consciousness,
I start realizing there is great harmony.
I start seeing the value in most things.
Then I start seeing the value in everything."

JOHN MORTON

Chapter Eight

THE BLESSING OF
OUR CONDITIONS

My dedication is that no matter what the condition, I love.

A S HUMAN BEINGS, we tend to create separations by making certain conditions more important than others, e.g., rich or poor, healthy or sick, happy or sad, etc. That is comparing. **My dedication is that no matter what the condition, I love.** That is what I am here to do. I love the condition because it comes from God, and I do not need to know anything more than that. It is blessed of God because it is of God.

I am not here to get into comparison or evaluation of the conditions. I am here to love the conditions, pure and simple. The fun becomes, how do I love them? How do I respond with my love? Let me count the ways, and let me find a new and better way to love each condition. If we are having a difficult time, let's look at the ways we are hanging on to what is no longer present and what no longer serves us.

One of the primary ways to love any condition is to be thankful for it. Start with gratitude, and realize that if an adjustment is needed, it is an internal adjustment. Do not castigate the outer condition by asking, "Why?" or "How dare you?" Those kinds of questions will take you into a sense of betrayal. If you say things like "I do not deserve this" or "I did not agree to this," you might as well look into the mirror and see that you are talking to yourself. Just consider that somehow all the conditions serve a purpose, perhaps to teach acceptance, patience, and new strength.

Just consider the possibility that when we approached the big condition that contains all conditions—called life—it was shown to us that there is really just one condition with a multitude of variations and that at some point we agreed to all of it. Even though it is quite common to argue, fight, or fuss, this reaction against any of the conditions present is just a demonstration of forgetfulness of the divine nature in all things. **When you go through the conditions—no matter how severe—in loving, you neutralize them and take authority over them.** Then you become one who walks free in each condition. You are not really troubled by the conditions because you have placed yourself in an unconditioned state of loving as you go through them.

Those words are easy to say, and it is a whole other level to live them and to put your flesh on them by putting your actions into a loving state. That takes God's participation in your life. God is the only one I know that can always do that. If you want to have the state that is unconditioned love and that is free of all of the conditions, whether positive or negative, you have to invoke your God, the God that can overcome all the conditions. That is a choice.

Part of the choice is appealing to God. You might ask, "God, are you ready?" Maybe God is not ready and responds, "Excuse me, I am still getting dressed. I did not have my breakfast yet. I did not get enough sleep last night." Can you imagine God responding like that? If you can, your God is too small. Those are just conditions. People can use any condition to decide, "I am not ready, I am not prepared, I am not going to. No! I refuse." Even that is a temporary condition because, sooner or later, something will happen and you will have to move. Your bowels will move, or you will need to take your next breath. You will not be able to avoid responding to the conditions present. If it is not one condition, it will be another, so you might as well handle your current condition with thankfulness and loving.

So we say, begin your day in a state of Light and love, the state of the Divine, so you are in contact with that as your reality throughout the day. That then becomes your choice and your dedication, so whatever condition meets or confronts you this day, you will choose into the unconditioned state of divine loving. If you forget, use that condition as an opportunity to choose back into the unconditioned state. It does not matter how many times you move into a condition as your reality or identification; it is just one more chance to choose into the unconditioned state of loving.

When you are ready, you really can choose the unconditional loving. Then you have greater confidence that you will make that choice each time, based on your experience.

If you keep making that choice in condition after condition, it becomes part of the field of who you are.

For a while, it may be that choice is like a little closet you are constantly going in and out of. Just to know you have a place inside of you that is an unconditioned state of loving is very important. The people who do not know that "go crazy," and their "craziness" tends to manifest in the nature of their struggles.

When we know the unconditioned state, we are in a state of peace. We are at ease. We have great confidence that God is with us. So the dark valley, or whatever you want to call the conditions that we walk through, has no real bearing on us because we walk in that state of the Divine.

As you invoke the Divine, you build it as a real field of awareness so you are at ease with all the conditions of life, all the shadows. It is a good idea to get a head start and build it up a little as conditions ebb and flow. **Take advantage of times when things are good to build up the unconditioned state inside yourself. Then, when the challenging conditions are flooding or seeming to overwhelm you, there will be a reservoir of loving strength you have built to withstand any outside conditions.** It may get very intense. It may be the kind of thing that tears you up emotionally, mentally, and every other way, except in your spirit. It cannot touch that, and when you know that, then you realize that **none of these conditions are going to get you or destroy you. None of them, including death, can compromise or destroy your spirit.**

When you build things up in the outer world, there are attachments, and some of them are very understandable, very human: "I love my family, and I want just certain kinds of conditions for my family, the ones that represent health, happiness, well-being, and prosperity. I want only these good things coming down that are the good conditions." You are deciding that there are bad conditions, and the reality of God is that they are all good. They are all useful. **No badness comes out of the Creator. We are the ones who make that and create that through our comparisons, interpretations, and judgments of the conditions.**

Even very negative conditions can be understood— though it may require much acceptance and patience—as aspects of God's grace, beauty, and love. They are not something to eliminate. God is not saying, "I made a mistake! I made a mistake! I have to get rid of these things!" They are there on purpose, and they serve a purpose that is divine.

Real progression is toward the positive. That is the progression that Spirit is on. In a way, it is a regression, because truly we are coming back, returning and letting go of where we have been to take on a greater reality.

In order to do that, we have to stay detached and unconditioned. If we do not, then we assign ourselves to our attachments and conditions. How long? As long as we assign ourselves. At some point we will realize it is unnecessary to do that. It is dumb. We realize, "I know better. I can do better. I see the better." Then we demonstrate that by our choices.

If you want health and prosperity, demonstrate that by being healthy and prosperous in the conditions you are in. If the conditions are severe, perhaps so severe that they seem to gnaw at you, then find a way to let the severity fill you. There is always something in any situation that can be used for betterment. At the very least, we can learn and apply the learning as understanding and wisdom.

Regardless of the nature of each experience, always let it pass. It may surprise you to learn that people hang on to experience by trying to analyze or understand. That just keeps the condition around by feeding it with your attention and energy.

Just let it go.

If you want to move past whatever situation you are in, simply let go and then direct yourself into the kind of situation you would like. If you want more admiration, make sure that the things you are doing are admirable to the people you are around. If you do not know what those things are, then ask. If you do not want to do what they say, go find people who are admiring what you want to be doing. If that means that you need to change and you do not want to change, then you had better get busy being happy in the situation you are in.

Ultimately, any situation is between you and God. And then it really becomes you as God. There is a merging, and that means a willingness to give up everything and everyone. You may not be prepared for that. You may say, "Well, I do not know if I am ready to give up all the conditions because the condition is my husband, the condition is my children, the condition is where I live. I like those conditions."

Jesus, as the Christ, said it in a particular way: "Anyone who loves his father or mother more than me is not worthy of me; anyone who loves his son or daughter more than me is not worthy of me; and anyone who does not take his cross and follow me is not worthy of me. Whoever finds his life will lose it, and whoever loses his life for my sake will find it."[1]

Was it an egotistical statement? Was Jesus saying, "I just want to control you and have you worship and follow me, because I am number one around here"? I do not see it that way. It is more like, "If you want to follow what I am doing and become part of it, it requires a great deal, perhaps everything you have to give. But you get to choose. Obviously, you have seen something, or you would not be interested. So if you have seen it, why not go toward the whole of it and find out what it is completely?"

If you are going to partake fully in the blessings, then trusting is essential. You can trust that the conditions in your life right now are on the straight and narrow, rather than thinking, "Oh, I made a big mistake," or "This cannot be on my path," or "This cannot be God's blessing manifesting." **The blessing comes when you accept, enjoy, and appreciate all conditions as somehow part of the great perfection for you on your path of awareness**

1. Matthew 10:37-39

toward God. It is a great day when you have overcome your fears, your conditions, and live instead in the unconditioned state of divine loving.

Baruch Bashan.

A Blessing of Simplicity

☙ LORD GOD, once again we ask to be more fully aware of
    your presence,
your Light, and your Sound that enfold us and nurture us.

In this moment, we are asking for your simplicity,
    the simple nature of who you are,
to be more revealed and apparent to us,
that we, too, may create in simple ways and in pure, clean
    ways.

So we ask that our conditioning toward wastefulness is lifted
    at this time,
that we willingly participate in clearing those things that no
    longer serve us.

And we ask that we become givers,
that we can give more than we receive,

and that what we receive is your bounty that comes through
the invisible in our heart as love,

> as truth,

> and as the joy of knowing that all is love,

> all is divine.

We ask you to visit us personally in this way,
so that we may have the willingness to move things on

> to a higher purpose

and to move things out of our surroundings,
according to your will.

Guide us for the highest good,
that we can be thankful always for what we find,
for who is with us in every moment.

We ask you to visit with our desires,
that they are lifted and directed once again on purpose,
through the Holy Spirit and through that which we know as

> our Soul.

Soothe our mind and our emotions.
Let your healing balm come to us physically.
And where we find pain and sorrow,
whether it be with ourselves or others,
let us soothe, that we bring comfort.

We are grateful for this moment of peace,

to experience your touch upon us,

knowing the perfection, the beauty in all things,

that we go forth smiling in your joy,

laughing that you play with us,

that we are here to delight.

And let us conduct our lives that we become friends—

friends of the Lord—

and friends to one another who love in the way of the Lord.

Baruch Bashan.

A Blessing of
the Oneness of God

I'd like you to consider that what you are doing in this blessing is experiencing what is already present. So you're not really doing anything. You're taking the energies of your consciousness and focusing them into what is present—what is present in truth, what is present in the reality of who you are and the reality of God.

&⁊ THIS BLESSING is a process of letting go. So wherever you are, let go.

Start with letting go of your body. Bring your consciousness around the body. Become aware of your skin, of the air around your skin. Now place your awareness into the body, however you do that. As your awareness moves into each part of your body, relax. That part lets go. It's as though you're caressing and embracing that part of you. Every part of you knows you are safe, you are loved and cared for, you are completely embraced. And so you let go, knowing there is no need to struggle. There's no harm here. There's just energy of loving and caring.

Place that loving and caring all though the body. Your body resonates in oneness. Your body is integrated in the Light. The presence of the Holy Spirit surrounds, fills, and protects you. You can completely let go.

Now this energy moves into your consciousness. The Light of loving and caring is with whatever you see or feel. It is with your thoughts, no matter what they are. Loving and caring are present. In every level of your consciousness, from the physical body into Spirit, there is just loving and caring.

You are the consciousness of loving and caring. In this consciousness, you are aware of the great diversity of God's creation. In this diversity, there is always loving and caring. This is the will of God—to love all the creation, in all of its forms, in all of who you are in your expressions and manifestations, and everything in the universe as well.

Bring your conscious awareness to the source of loving and caring. And bring that source to your body, to this physical world.

Prepare a place for God's will. God's will is growing in you. If there are any remaining concerns that you have—worries, fears, or doubts about any aspect of your life—there is only loving and caring. In this moment and place, let there only be loving and caring.

You become the source of loving and caring.

You are blessed in the oneness of God.

Baruch Bashan.

تا که بی این همه بسه با تو دم زنم

"*Love conquers all things;*
let us too surrender to Love."

VIRGIL

Chapter Nine

THE BLESSING OF
CHOOSING LOVING

*This world is designed to bring lessons—
and not necessarily comfortable ones.*

PERHAPS YOU WERE BORN into an environment where you were surrounded by loving. Your mother and father were loving, the doctor was loving, the nurses were loving, whoever was there when you came into the world was loving. **No matter how we come into the world or how great the presence of loving has been, there is always a greater loving to come into our expression.**

This world is designed to bring lessons—and not necessarily comfortable ones. Each lesson presents an opportunity to experience and express the loving that is already present. That is not a secret or even a revelation. But at some point we will know that loving is always present, even if we do not want to admit it to ourselves and do many things to deny it.

Perhaps another extreme was present as you came into the world: your parents appeared unloving, a doctor slapped you and appeared harsh or violent, etc. This world can appear cold, hostile, tyrannical, or alien.

At some point we may begin forming an attitude that could be called unloving. Here's the bad news: As we form an attitude of unloving toward anything or anyone, we are actually forming that attitude toward ourselves.

One of the ways our "unloving" can be recognized is as a hardness that comes into our consciousness. As hardness comes into our being, we can become callous and insensitive. As we become more insensitive, our perceptions portray a harsh and painful world. It then becomes easier to adopt an attitude toward the world resulting in our experiencing and in turn expressing more harshness, negativity, and pain.

Occasionally a person can go all the way through their life gradually becoming more hardened and harsh as a way of dealing with the world. That is very rare because usually somewhere along the way, there is a visitation, a moment when no matter how dark or how cloudy or stormy it is, the sunlight gets through and touches us, reminding us that there is more to this world than the darkness, harshness, or storms.

In our process of dealing with the world, we play two sides. One side we refer to as the negative, the painful, or the disturbing. The other side is the loving, the light, and the beautiful. As we learn to play this game between the two sides, we realize that one is more of our nature. Perhaps we see it as more of the way we would like to be. In other words, we can look upon ourselves as actually being unloving, dark, or "deep down inside, no good." We can still realize, however, that underneath our negative picture of ourselves is the desire to be good.

No matter what attitude we form in relationship to the polarities we find in the world, we are still called upon to make choices. There is no way to remove ourselves from the choices that are here. There is decision by "default" or "slide," but that is still a choice that will have real consequences. In each moment, we are always making a choice to be more loving or more unloving.

A while back, as I was out walking, I became aware of a message about loving. It was an affirmation: "I am increasing the loving. I am increasing the loving." I kept hearing this message: "I am increasing the loving." It was as if the message was coming from the outside and also from inside me. I realized that this message is an affirmation for each moment of each day of my life. **We all have a primary responsibility to increase our loving each day.** That realization was humbling to me because I realized that I do not always do that with my attitude and choices even when it is my intention.

As I walked, I considered how the source of loving is inexhaustible. There is no way we can ever exhaust the opportunity to be more loving. Part of the illusion that I was carrying around was that the source of loving is finite. Somehow I had formed an idea that we have the ability to take away from the loving, to make it less than what it is. My experience was teaching me that the source of loving is always full. It is more than full. **The supply of loving goes**

beyond anything or anyone that uses it, no matter how much is required.

Loving is what life is about, and this world is designed to reflect a process for increasing the loving. There is not a real difference between what life is about and what loving is about. They are synonymous. When we have our perceptions and our experiences that try to say that "life is less than loving" or "life is an aberration from what real loving is," those are just messages that say we are not fully aware of what loving is.

As we encounter what life is, we encounter loving. And as we encounter what God is, we encounter loving. That is a process that starts transcending where we find ourselves. It starts transcending what meets us in terms of the physicality of this world and starts allowing us to transcend into another world that is of the Spirit. The loving starts becoming something that is all-encompassing, and we realize that we are loving. The loving is more than what we think or feel or how we relate to the people and circumstances in our life.

At the point we experience our loving encompassing all things, we become aware that we are more than what we perceive. We are more than what we experience. Then we are at a point where we are reaching into God and having God reveal the fullness of what life is. This is when the spirit in our consciousness is coming into a greater maturity. This is when we start questing for a greater reality, a greater knowing of what loving is, what God is, and who we are.

It is then that a consciousness that guides your awareness to the truth can come forward, revealing the action of God that is living truth and the loving of God. It then becomes a process of you surrendering to the truth that sets you free.

If you are deciding that your life is based on unloving, then you are in very treacherous territory, and the downfall from your illusions is imminent. Stop right there. Go no further until you are once again relating to loving in people and things. Let "loving in all ways" be your dedication, your affirmation. It is the most vital part of what we are doing in this world. It does not require a signature from the world. It does not require proof. You can know that you are blessed that you even recognize loving, and you can be grateful to know that loving is the way that you have chosen to live your life.

I have had lots of experiences of moving away from the loving and moving back into the loving. Moving back into the loving is all that really counts. When you realize this, then more and more you will be choosing loving and finding loving in your experience and expression.

Loving is a unified action of God that harmonizes and overcomes whatever separation we may find. We stand in with its celebration. As we step forward, there is a greater celebration, and the loving increases. And no matter what happens, we are choosing a celebration of loving.

Baruch Bashan.

A Blessing of Choosing Loving

❧ LORD GOD, we give thanks that we have brought
ourselves to this place of restoration.

We give thanks for our willingness to choose back, to take our
place with our Soul. We recognize this is a constant choice in
this world, to choose back into the Spirit, so we openly, willingly choose the loving, choose the forgiving.

And we ask your assistance right now to place this as a
    dedication,
that we will sustain the focus of loving, that we will overcome
all those things that try and test us in our judgments, in our
resistance, in our forgetting that we are divine.

We ask for the gift of spiritual discernment,
    that we can see and know those things that are of your will,
    bypassing what is unnecessary,

letting go of what no longer serves us, holding understanding and acceptance toward all that appears less than divine.

And in all of this, we affirm our choosing back to the loving that is the hallmark of your presence.

Baruch Bashan.

A Blessing of
Dedication to God

Take in a few deep breaths to relax yourself more.

When you breathe in, there's an energy of ease and relaxation that comes in on the breath, and as you breathe out, you let go of tension. You breathe out any negative concerns that you have, so that through breathing deeply, you can come into a greater sense of harmony with everything. And you can let go of judgments, any againstness that you've been holding onto, whether conscious or unconscious.

In this process, we again ask for the Light, the Light that comes through the Holy Spirit, surrounding, protecting, and filling you, allowing just what is for the highest good.

For a moment, just consider yourself as having been on a long journey. It doesn't matter so much where you've been as to realize where you are and how you are feeling. Maybe you're aware that you're tired or that you have a sense of exhaustion. You may feel places in your body where there is pain or stress, and you'd like to have some rest, to let go of the long journey.

So let yourself come to a place where you can get cleaned up, bathe, put on new clothes. If you're hungry, you will be fed. If you're thirsty, there's plenty to drink.

All of what happens to you now is to remove the stress, the tiredness, to remove the dirt and grime, to release this sense of a long journey, to release it from your body.

Now experience a most beautiful energy that has a way of cleansing you all the way into your cells. This is an inner and outer cleansing.

This radiant energy is now working with you more and more. It lovingly purifies, integrates, harmonizes. You become more aware of the divine blessing.

You can also be aware of assistance that you are receiving, that there are those who would assist you, to heal and strengthen you. Those who assist you in this are your friends, even intimate in friendship, and you experience that you are loved, you are honored, you are cherished for who you are.

You may want to protest the love because of what you've done and what you've been through, and you might consider yourself not worthy of love. Yet no matter what you reveal about yourself, about your journey, you are loved. You're cared for as the Beloved. You don't have to understand how anyone could love you the way you are; they just do.

Now, you are feeling the most beautiful sense of wholeness, of being rested and nourished. Your vitality is restored, and all you consider you can now appreciate.

You now understand the value in all of your experience. And whatever comes to mind that you've held as an againstness, as some form of judgment, you forgive. As things come to mind, forgiveness is instantly present. It happens so powerfully, so rapidly, that you have no opportunity to remember what has been forgiven. So it is truly forgiven and forgotten. The content no longer has meaning. There is nothing that is not forgiven. The forgiveness is present as soon as you allow it, as soon as you open to it.

Others may come to mind, those whom you have judged, those whom you have condemned, those whom you have had ill thoughts and feelings toward. Where there has been hatred, loving soothes you. Loving transforms the thoughts of those whom you have judged and condemned.

Where you have punished, love and mercy is now your way. That is now what is bestowed. So all are forgiven, all are set free inside of you. There's simply no place for againstness inside you. There is peace toward all—the peace that surpasses understanding, the peace above and beyond all things. All becomes a cause for peace, for love, for the liberation of the Spirit.

If you do not know how to forgive and forget, you can call forward the One whose nature is to forgive all, to love all, the One who is anointed in this purpose of God, by God. It is at your service. It can forgive what you do not know how to forgive, love what you do not know how to love, and take away the anguish that has visited your mind and emotions, the places in your body where you've harbored the resentment, the disappointment, the guilt. All forms of negativity are now loved and forgiven by this Holy One.

And so the love, the Light of God is upon you. You now open yourself to receive fully, that no place in your body, mind, or Soul is without love, without peace.

Drink in the overflow of love and joy of the Spirit of God. You now have the ability to view all things—all things in this world and your life and all things about yourself—through the eyes of love, the eyes that see peace and understanding. The wisdom of God is upon you.

And in this moment, you have the opportunity to make a decision, a commitment to dedicate yourself to the love of God, the blessings of God, that already are upon you.

You realize that this commitment involves your continual choosing to refuse to judge, to hold anyone, any situation, in a place of negativity, that from now on, you are dedicated to love, to peace, to harmony.

And when you forget your divine commission, you forgive. You forget about what has happened, and you move forward, dedicating yourself again and anew to the love of God, the love that surpasses all things, the blessings that already are.

Baruch Bashan.

تا کی این همه بارهٔ نسیه با تو دم زنم

136   "I gave my Soul to Him
        And all the things I owned were His:
        I have no flock to tend
        Nor any other trade
        And my one ministry is love."

        ST. JOHN of the CROSS

Chapter Ten

THE BLESSING OF LIFTING
TO GOD'S STANDARDS

Our task is to stop making choices that limit
and start making choices that manifest the blessings.

T HERE IS A HIGHER STANDARD of living available to us, which we can attain, that I call practical spirituality.

This is not something that we just study or analyze or that was lived at some distant time that we reminisce or wonder about. If we cannot practice our spirituality, if we are not able to live beyond the pulpit and express into the world, then it just does not mean much, if anything. If spirituality has no real application, then it tends to be simply a nice idea or a romantic fantasy.

Once, while I was in South America, I was watching television reports on the famine in Somalia, and it became very clear that I should go there myself. I was looking at what was occurring not as an individual situation but as a situation perpetuating itself into an entire nation and demanding the attention of the world.

The tremendous pull to go was generated by the level of response that I personally experienced as insufficient. The technology of modern television was bringing me face to face with needless and massive human suffering. If the eye of the camera could get close, then so could a helping hand. Within my consciousness, I saw that just one person could make the needed difference.

I asked myself, "What is so important about what I'm doing that I couldn't travel to Somalia and stand up for a higher standard of life?" It was not just to "drop everything and go," though the impulse was to do exactly that. I needed to look at my level of responsibility with the Spirit of God that I worship and allow myself to experience what was there for me to do in response.

This look at my personal level of responsibility for a situation that seemed so overwhelming and remote was quite daunting. But my personal responsibility to the Somalian situation was undeniable and imminent even with what appeared to me as very substantial personal responsibilities and commitments, such as my family and work.

Often when we see the kind of human suffering that was occurring in Somalia, we want to turn away—sometimes uncontrollably—when we are faced by the severity of what we feel from witnessing the conditions of others' suffering. How are we to determine what our level of responsibility is when we are confronted by such massive needs in our world?

A quandary is always an occasion to look inside for the counsel of God or whatever you use for your reference of the highest standards. On the one hand, in the midst of others' suffering, we can often perceive a lack of response in relation to those who appear to have and those who have not. We can feel the pull to respond, to help somehow. On the other hand, suffering is not pleasant for anyone, so why bring the suffering to ourselves by getting involved in situations that appear to be not personally of our own making?

Three days later I was still considering that I should go to Somalia. I began to seriously consider the implications of actually going to Somalia, the impact on my family, my work, and the rest of my involvements. What would I have to do in order to go? When would I go? Would I still go if certain conditions improved? Knowing that emotions—including mine—have cycles and shifts, I chose to wait two weeks before making a decision.

At last, the governments of certain countries, particularly the United States with support from a United Nations resolution, opted for military intervention to ensure that people would get the food and basic assistance they so desperately needed. I cannot think of a better use of the military than to ensure the safety and welfare of a desperate people, through mobilizing and protecting the delivery of food, supplies, and assistance to those who are most in need.

And so with the evidence that what was needed was being done, I did not go to Somalia. But it is the kind of situation that continues to affect me, as well it should. I am still very much affected by situations in the world that appear to lack human kindness and compassion. Pictures of emaciated, starving people, young and old, raging inhumanity and violence, degradation of the environment, and so on are clearly not to be ignored if we are to live in a world of health, wealth, and happiness.

Regardless of who these people are and what they have created for themselves, especially the children, our human compassion implores us to do something to help. We all deserve better, and we can have better.

The question we all have to consider is, what is the level of response called for when a situation moves us to do something?

There are certain people who look at the situation and pose a different set of questions. "Somalia or Kosovo is a distant, unrelated situation. Why don't we take care of the people in our own backyard who are suffering, are without food or shelter, are in poor health, and need assistance? I'm sure there are people close by in our communities who need assistance."

So true.

The situations, and more so the consciousness, of the people in need confront all of us who are witnesses to create a higher standard of living. The greatest opportunity to raise the standard will be found at the place where it is the lowest. When we witness what is being shown to us in places like Somalia or Kosovo on such a massive scale, we can realize that we can well afford to do something from our place of living at a much higher standard. In one sense, we cannot afford not to respond, lest by our denial we relegate ourselves to a lower standard.

We could take a viewpoint of great altitude to see the causes in the situation resulting from all the levels of choice. We could take a position that these people have all chosen the conditions in which they live in order to justify our doing nothing in response. Yes, we could be right. But is there a higher standard of living to attain? And are there those who have already demonstrated that a higher standard can be attained? Are we willing to subscribe to the higher standard of living?

One of the primary standards of living that God reveals to us is to love with abandon. That means to love without any holds that would restrict the loving, including distance, culture, or any resulting costs. It could mean to give up everything that holds us back from fully loving, fully caring, and fully doing what we can to lift the situation to a higher standard.

We may need to abandon our previous standards of loving that are bound by our comforts, our morality, our beliefs, or whatever else keeps us from freely loving. As we practice our spirituality, we are bound to learn how to move past standards of loving that are limited by separation, prejudice, and fear.

Loving is God's way. When loving makes its way known to us, we are to follow with abandon and to do so boldly, without reservation. When John-Roger administered my blessing to set me aside to perform ordinations as a minister, I was told, "It is the unconditionalness of life that must be lived." We are to abandon the smaller self that we have previously known, for the larger Self that is God's unconditional nature, boundless in love, boundless in its ability to overcome any restriction.

Recently, a student from a university I am involved with was leaving a weekend class when she was hit by a car while walking in a crosswalk. The accident resulted in some severe broken bones and internal injuries. All things considered, she is now doing fine. An occurrence of this magnitude, of course, affects her family, friends, and fellow students. When something like this happens, we send all those involved God's Light for healing and whatever else is needed. And we have a responsibility to raise the standard, perhaps with traffic controls, so this kind of event is less likely to happen.

These kinds of occurrences happen as part of our life experience in this world. Each time we are "hit," we can immediately abandon whatever might close us down to the opportunity to extend loving and caring to all those affected by the situation. This is especially true whenever life brings us unexpected hits to overcome. We must learn to abandon the urge to react negatively with our upset and interpretations against the situations. We must learn to abandon any standards that could allow us to judge people and situations as anything like evil or a cause to wreak havoc and violence. We are called upon to consider how we can stop whatever is lowering God's standards by which we live.

If, together, we are to bring forward a higher standard of living and loving, then we must be willing to remain open and compassionate toward the suffering of others. **For in the midst of human suffering is always a great opportunity to witness and assist with the outpouring of the Spirit of God to all.** If we are to experience the greater oneness with the Spirit inwardly, then we must remain open to support our connection outwardly as well. We must be willing to do unto others what God, through the Spirit, would do through us as the expression.

We must abandon whatever standards would keep us from living according to the Spirit, to be the vessel of God's intention through us.

We are learning how to abandon outmoded standards so we may participate in manifesting God's love onto the planet. By doing this, we will generate the necessary energy and responses from the Light to wherever people are crying out. **As we are willing to make the blessings of loving, caring, and sharing manifest, then other blessings that are available in Spirit will manifest as greater health, wealth, happiness, etc. This is grace in action.**

If you are going to dedicate yourself to a more spiritual life, then it follows that you are going to dedicate yourself to a higher standard of living and loving. Does this translate into your having better furniture, better food on the table, better clothes, a nicer car, and nicer friends? Sure, that can be part of it. It is about a better standard of living in all aspects of your life. With God, we are dealing with an unlimited source with unlimited possibilities.

There is something further that goes with a dedication to raising the standard of living in all aspects of our

145

life: a decision to choose into a higher standard of living in *every* aspect of life.

It begins with you and it ends with you. It includes everything in between as well. As you continue to raise the standards by which you live your life, you will have greater responsibility to abide by the higher standards. There are sacrifices that go with this, challenges that will confront you in raising the standards, requiring patience and your willingness to change from the lower standards.

Simply stated, you must subscribe to and be willing to maintain greater standards in everything you do, regardless of the conditions and especially with a willingness to let go of the past. Are you willing to let go of the past?

What you subscribe to right now—by the way you live from now on—determines what your standards of living become.

By worshiping God within, we automatically adopt the higher standards of living that our spiritual transformation will bring forward. It is important to realize that God will transform your life as promised in scriptures when you seek "first the kingdom of God … and all these things shall be added unto you."[1] God is the one who commands us to abandon all else so that we can then seek his kingdom. In the process of abandoning everything to God, we place ourselves in a direct line to receive the divine inheritance that is our destiny while we are living here in the world.

1. MATTHEW 6:33

We are to learn how to act in accordance with the blessings of God, that they may become manifest.

One of the miracles of God is that there is room for every one of us to be in this direct line to receive the blessings that are our divine inheritance. We can and do share in the higher standards of living that God has already placed in Spirit as all the blessings that await our partaking. We have direct access to the blessings now. **Our task is to stop making choices that limit and start making choices that manifest the blessings.** As we each do this for ourselves individually, we will do this for one another, because the blessings are designed to be shared. The more we raise our own standards, the more the standards are raised for one another and all of us together.

Raising the standards begins right where you live. Make sure you are taking care of the basic standards. The basic standards are things like paying your bills, taking care of your body, cleaning your teeth, kissing your children good-night, getting along with your neighbors, and generally leaving situations better than you found them. Learn to make the most of and enjoy what you already have.

Manifesting the blessings is not really anything that is complicated or even difficult. Clear out what is not serving you or no longer actively being utilized. Give and share joyously. Receive graciously. Make amends. Adorn yourself first with inner beauty so the outer beauty may benefit from your best intentions. Contribute more than you take. Make each place you

147

find yourself better than you found it. Be an abundant source of good tidings to and from God. In short, let go and let God.

Baruch Bashan.

A Blessing of
the Lord, Thy God

❧ WE MAY CALL UPON GOD as our Lord—and I mean
this personally for each one of us as direct communication,
communion—and God may increasingly call upon us in kind.
I love the term Lord as a way to refer to God because it's
both personal and impersonal all at once. The Lord signifies
one who is of a higher or even the highest state and who is
among us or with us in a personal, direct way.

Regardless of your personal faith, consider that our true Lord
is one who is a mutual friend, a friend to all—a Lord who is
an ultimate master and also an ultimate servant to each of us.
We get to both follow and be followed by the same one. Our
Lord absolutely maintains the highest standards, which are
incorruptible. Would you want a Lord who was corrupt, who
lied and deceived, or who betrayed and sold you out?

Not when you have an immaculate Lord, one whom we can perfectly lead and whom we can follow into the Spirit.

How well do you know the Lord, thy God? Are you willing to raise your standards to the standards of the Lord? Are you willing to come close to the Lord's countenance, to come into the very presence that transmits the Divine directly unto you?

As humans, when we subscribe to the Lord's standards of living, we mess up regularly, choosing misalignment instead of and in spite of our best intentions. By our ignorance and out of desperate pain or fear, we may have attempted to mock, spite, or curse the Lord. Thank God that the Lord's presence is incorruptible and indestructible. The Lord that we are working with does not "smite thee" for your reaction or your cursing. There is a law of reality that makes sure all of our creations are accounted for so that what we sow, we shall reap. We are responsible for our actions, so by our choices, our life manifests.

The Lord of us all, having already overcome the world, is a consciousness full of grace and forgiveness for our transgressions, who has demonstrated and shows us how to transcend what we have created or miscreated as the case may be. Just as deep in the heart of every parent toward their child, the Lord loves each one of us regardless of what we turn out to become.

Authentic spirituality is a living worship that follows you out the door. Wherever you go, you are in worship. The way you will most know this is when you are alone and think that nobody is around. That is when you know about your level of relationship to the Lord. You may consider that since the Lord is going to forgive you, you can lower your standards or cheat.

You don't really mock the Lord, but you can mock yourself. You might consider which self would be mocked. Mocking in this case is an attempt to mimic or imitate. The false self, not the Lord or your true self, is the one who is mocked by attempts to cheat and not uphold the higher standards of living available to us as choices. Attempts to do so backfire on the instigator.

I have a message for you. You can decide from whom it comes:

I love you.
I am always with you.
Be open to the Light and Sound you sense.
Listen to your heart, for that is where I am.

I love to be close with you, to just take you in my arms, and I would like you to take me in your arms, so we can embrace. We don't have to have a reason.

You do not have to show me how good you are. I already know it. You were made good. Good is all we are together. We do not bother to do anything less than good.

There is a place prepared. We will do what we can to make your life better and give you what you came here for.

I can do as much as you allow. I have a lot of help. The consciousness that I am is always present, always around you. That's the consciousness you are. We are doing this together.

Your life is a gift; give it freely, with abandon. When you are at your worst, I am at my best. Be patient. Things are always working for the best. Do your part.

When you see the Lord, catch up. The Lord is prepared to go with you and goes wherever you go. There is nothing wrong with this world. It is absolutely perfect. Do not be concerned by what you see or by what disturbs you. Just know that it is a call to come in, lift, and be involved in the work of the Lord.

Baruch Bashan.

A Blessing of Peace

ᥰᏸ LORD GOD, we ask your blessing of Light, through the
Christ and Holy Spirit, surrounding and protecting and
filling each one of us gathered here, that you sanctify this
place and each one of us so we can release any negativity
into this Light, becoming instruments of the Light anchoring
into the earth, into its very core, radiating as a column up
through where we are gathered here and radiating around
this place, to the people, to whatever is here that can absorb
and be transformed in the Light.

We see this Light radiating, illuminating, making all
beautiful, clean, and clear. We see it in the very smallest
ways and in the greatest way affecting all, so the entire planet
is illuminating and radiating through the Light of the Holy
Spirit, as the presence of peace comes into greater
manifestation.

We, in our simple humanity, are here to serve, that in this moment, we offer ourselves as instruments of your peace and your loving action. We surrender our will into your will, that you know what is best. You know the hearts and the troubles of all. You know what the Light must do and can do. We give ourselves freely. We ask for a change of consciousness toward the highest good of all concerned, that this action take place at the highest rate and the greatest way, so that grace is being extended. May we be part of a new peace, the one spoken of long ago, a peace of God, where all is unified in love and harmony, that we call it forward this day and forever more.

And now let our voices sing out in your name, that we become your holy vibration, the one that is heard by all those you have called, all who have known you face to face. Let us become that holy vibration and sound, radiating like a spring that issues forth in purity, that bathes all in your Light and love, healing all, forgiving all, making all anew, that we rejoice here in celebration, that we hear a holy chorus, a celestial melody singing out.

Let us become your silence.

And we hear you say, "Peace unto you, Beloved.
Peace unto all."

Baruch Bashan.

تا که بی این همه با تو دم زنم

156

"By participation in Christ we become Christ's."

ROGER BACON

Chapter Eleven

THE BLESSING OF THE

ANOINTING OF GOD

When Spirit takes one, it takes us all.

A S WE WAKE UP TO THE LIGHT, we begin to direct our focus more into the Light. This can be as simple as doing something good in the world. As we contact the Source of Light, we can bring more Light into the world and into ourselves physically. That's the practice of moving with God and Spirit: to contact that Source of Light.

This contact and connection represents a consciousness that goes to God. It goes all the way. What does that consciousness (or energy) do when it gets to the earth? It manifests materially through a form such as a body.

That is how it starts. It takes just one. But **when Spirit takes one, it takes us all.** That is how it functions. It is a consciousness of all going to God. As we contact that consciousness, there is the opportunity for returning our awareness more fully to the Soul and transcending all negativity.

This complete contact has already been achieved by, among others, Jesus the Christ. Although there were others before him, it was for Jesus to establish access to the Soul level. Once he did this, it was done for all Souls. All Souls are saved. Not one Soul is lost. Prior to that point, we were confined to our negativity, and we had to personally undo our negativity and pay our debts before we could gain access to the higher awareness of God. We were bound to the law of cause and effect and karma. That is the Law of Moses: "An eye for an eye, and a tooth for a tooth."[1] Jesus, by the anointing of God, brought forward grace and the potential of entry into the Soul realm for all.

160

We do not control access to God. We just participate. However you manage to do it, do it! That is an advertisement for God, for your spiritual heritage, and for your Soul. If you can find a way, just do it.

I am here to say that there is a way. I am dedicated to it, and because there is that dedication, it is like I am knocking on the door and saying, "God, can I come home now?" Through the Christ, it was set up so the door had to open and so that no Soul asking for the Light could be refused.

We are told that Jesus died for our sins. That is an interpretation. The understanding of the crucifixion reveals the love that will sacrifice all things in this world and that our Soul is not destroyed. I consider that it is more accurate to say that Jesus lives for our Soul. As Souls, we are to release ourselves from our transgressions and accept the anointing of God that is the true "Christening" by the one who anoints us. That is the

---

1. MATTHEW 5:38; EXODUS 21:24

meaning of the Hebrew term *messiah*. It is really saying, "I accept my anointing of God."

Personally, I love the idea of taking the anointing. The ritual of anointing is often associated with the area of the head, typically with an oil that has been blessed. Do you think it is the oil, or do you suppose it is the energy that does the anointing? And from where or whom does the energy of anointing come?

When an anointing is done for one, it is also available for those who present themselves. You make your head available, while in reality, all parts of you are to be anointed. At the Last Supper with his Disciples, Jesus anointed their feet—usually one of the most unclean parts of the body. As Jesus did this, Peter put up a protest: "Lord, you shouldn't be washing my feet," and Jesus said, in effect, "If I cannot wash your feet, then you cannot take what I have to give you." Peter then responded something like, "If that's the way it is, then wash not just my feet but all of me."[2] That is the true anointing, from head to toe, and everything in between.

What is the anointing? It is blessing the body and blessing the consciousness to its original state, the state of God in the highest. It is removing what is unclean or impure. This is the Christ anointing. When it happened to Jesus, a voice said, "This is my beloved Son, in whom I am well pleased."[3] It doesn't matter what your

2. JOHN 13:4-9
3. MATTHEW 3:17

gender is. Whether you are female or male does not have any more significance in Spirit than the flip of a coin. If, in order to receive your anointing you had to "convert" from a male to a female or vice versa, would you accept or protest? Consider the change needed to become clean and pure.

When Jesus stepped in with the woman who was to be stoned and said, "Whoever is without sin throw the first stone," he knew what the outcome would be. He knew that as human beings, we all sin. We all have imperfections. That is not an issue with God; in fact, it is part of the divine plan. We came into imperfection when we came into a world of negativity. What's important in this story is what happened when no one threw a stone.

Jesus asked the woman, "Did they judge you?"

"No," was her reply.

Jesus then said to her, "Neither have I judged you. Get up and sin no more."[4]

We may think, "That's easy for you to say, Jesus." However, that is the order of the anointing. Even though we would want to fully take on our perfection, as human beings we remain imperfect. I have my imperfections. I have my transgressions. I'm human. We're all human.

Sometimes people try to make a demand on me. They will say things like, "Oh, you're supposed to be spiritual. You teach people to be spiritual. Therefore, you're perfect." I am a spiritual being expressing, also, as a human

---

4. JOHN 8:3-11

being. I'm human, but I know where my worship is. My worship is in the perfection of the Spirit, of the Soul in me. I declare myself perfected by God, and so are you. God does the work, and he's not finished. God is not done with me yet, so don't interfere because perfection is on the way. On this level, my life is about completion. A blessed life is a complete life. A blessing that has been placed upon your life is like a seed that is planted: Be patient and let yourself grow to completion.

163

Baruch Bashan.

A Blessing of the Christ

WE DO not have to renounce our past.
We actually must acknowledge it in full,
as if to say, "I did it all."
And we surrender ourselves into the Christ,
as a blessing to live in the truth that is God's unconditional
love,

> forgiving all,
>
> accepting all,
>
> blessing all.

And if we accept the challenge to go forward in the Christ,
we dedicate ourselves to the life of unconditional love,
to forgiving all,
a life that lifts wherever we are,
that sees the good in all people and situations,
that we trust in God, the provider of all,

the source of infinite supply,

    infinite good,

who restores us when we are tired,

strengthens us in our weakness,

heals us in our pain.

We are those who make straight the way for the Lord.

It does not matter how we have conducted ourselves up to now,

    for the Christ comes to those who have sinned and

      transgressed.

We breathe in this Holy Spirit.

We breathe out our forgiveness of all things.

We breathe in our joy.

We breathe out our sadness and hardship, letting it all go.

We breathe in God's peace, and we breathe out this peace toward all.

Now consider yourself in communion with the Lord,

that you can say whatever you like

and listen to the words the Lord speaks.

Perhaps you will hear the Lord say,

"Loving is the Way."

Begin it inside,

that's the inner way,

and while you're in the world, practice God's love.

It's not enough to see the face of God.

Live that reality.

That's when you will realize yourself in the face of God.

To love somebody is to see the face of God.

Baruch Bashan.

"Inside this clay jug there are canyons
        and pine mountains, and the maker of canyons and
            pine mountains!
All seven oceans are inside, and hundreds of millions
        of stars.
The acid that tests gold is there, and the one
        who judges jewels.
And the music from the strings no one touches, and the
        source of all water.
If you want the truth, I will tell you the truth:
Friend, listen: the God whom I love is inside."

KABIR

Chapter Twelve

THE BLESSING OF
GOD'S PRESENCE

*Perhaps we can skip the journey of looking for our essence outside
ourselves, accept that it is inside, and simply sit down,
go inside, and experience enlightenment.*

T HE MOVIE *BROTHER SUN, SISTER MOON* is the story of St. Francis of Assisi. At one point in the film, St. Francis says, "We are a band of men who are lovers of God." I feel empathy not only with that statement attributed to St. Francis but also with something much deeper and more difficult to put into words.

Those of us directly involved with Spirit are lovers of God—the one God of us all. In other words, once we awaken to the Spirit of God, we become lovers of God. In the Bible, we are told, "God is love; and he that dwelleth in love dwelleth in God, and God in him."[1] That translates to "the indwelling God in each of us loves all of creation"— everyone and everything without exception. The worst sinner is loved by the indwelling God. The most despicable human being is loved by the indwelling God. God sets a great example that we are all reaching toward, which is to love all of creation without exception. Jesus, when he physi-

---

1. 1 JOHN 4:16

cally walked the earth, certainly was one example of some-one who lived his life this way. There are many others.

What good are the life story and teachings of Jesus the Christ, or any other example of God living through the human form, if they are not applicable to us individually? If they belong only to a time that is dead and gone, then they are virtually a waste of our time to consider. A major part of the significance of the life of Christ goes well beyond the redemption from the transgressions of our existence in this world. The life of Christ is a demonstration of how the Spirit—or Holy Spirit—lives in the flesh, the human form. The message of the Christ is to love one another and all things, as God in the flesh within each of us would love in return. **The Christ lives continuously in each moment through our willingness to love unconditionally.**

The opportunity to claim the blessings of God is present here and now. It is within reach and catchable. It is alive. Are you conducting your life in such a way that you are bringing the blessings more alive? Or are you conducting life in such a way that the blessings appear to be non-existent, feeble, or weak?

You have the potential to fully awaken to the blessings within you and to bring blessings alive into your consciousness and your life's expression. You awaken to the blessings by moving into your indwelling spiritual awareness.

The Bible I grew up with talks about where God is found. It is the same place the kingdom of God is found.

"The kingdom of God is within you,"[2] and "God is a Spirit and they that worship him must worship him in spirit and in truth."[3] What is taking place in this world is an inner process. Let's see if we can demonstrate that.

Where are you reading these words right now?

On the paper outside of you? If you close your eyes, what happens? You won't see the words unless, of course, you have the ability to retain the image of the paper for your mind to "see." That is because you actually experience within yourself what you see. When you close your eyes, you stop seeing the printed words on the paper because *where* you see the printing is inside of you. *Where* you experience life is inside. You experience God inside. **What if God's big joke is to hide inside you and everything else in the world?**

Siddhartha, the Buddha, went on a long journey in search of God, the essence of life, and became very tired of the process. One day he more or less quit and sat down against a tree. Then, what he was looking for appeared. In that moment, he received the enlightenment he was looking for. **Perhaps we can skip the journey of looking for our essence outside ourselves, accept that it is inside, and simply sit down, go inside, and experience enlightenment.**

Locating our inner spiritual awareness is not unlike what Siddhartha went through. It is a process of letting go

173

2. LUKE 17:21
3. JOHN 4:24

of the outer world and going into the inner worlds, or the inner experience.

When we call ourselves forward in the Light (which I described in Chapter 2), we're asking for a greater presence of Spirit. It is a kind of joke because the God we are dealing with is the one who is omnipresent and always present. **How can God come** *more* **present if It is already omnipresent? Perhaps the reality is that we become more present. When** *we* **become more present, God becomes more present in our experience.**

The real joke is when we think God is not present and our request or our prayer is along the lines of, "God, stop what you are doing so you can come on over here and pay some attention to me." Sometimes we approach God as the "bellhop in the sky," as if God is under our command rather than that we are under the command of God. And even though the greater truth is that we are under God's command, whenever we call out, whatever we do, God watches, listens, and responds.

When we say an invocation ("call in the Light"), we call out to God, asking for a particular presence of God. Then we get to experience whether or not that presence takes place. If we then initiate a process of chanting the name of God, such as with Ani-Hu (an ancient name for God, pronounced "An-I-Hugh"), we are acknowledging that we know the name of God. That is a very bold proposition. As a result of calling out God's name, does God come more present? The answer is that it is entirely between you and God. Regardless of what anyone else may experience, you have your own direct experience with God.

Locating spiritual awareness is an experience of going to the greatest part of God and integrating with your true self. The opposite of this is attempting to be something that you are not, which we have all done at various points in our lives. This goes with the process of being human and is indicative of worshiping something less than the God within yourself.

Thank God there is forgiveness and one who can pardon us. We say "pardon me" when we make a mistake. That is like saying "forgive me." If I walk into an elevator and step on somebody's foot, I might say, "Pardon me," or "Forgive me." It is a recognition that I stepped where I should not have stepped, and I'm attempting to balance the error of my ways.

We want our own errors to be forgiven, but are we willing to forgive the errors of others? Some people conduct their lives this way: "If you cut me off in traffic, I'm going to cut you off in traffic." That's reverting to an archaic way of life called "an eye for an eye and a tooth for a tooth."[4] It is also the law that binds us into this world and convicts us to some form of punishment, "for all they that take the sword shall perish by the sword."[5]

We are striving to live under grace when we ask for forgiveness and give forgiveness. Are there exceptions? Not

4. MATTHEW 5:38; EXODUS 21:24
5. MATTHEW 26:52

unless we want to fall under the law that would bind us. Scripture tells us, "Judge not, and you shall not be judged. Condemn not, and you shall not be condemned. Forgive, and you will be forgiven."[6] We forgive unconditionally, as God forgives us unconditionally.

There are some things people believe are unpardonable or unforgivable, and they often elect themselves as the judge, jury, and executioner. Whenever people judge against others or themselves, they are being very presumptuous. The presumption is, "I know enough about your life on all levels and for all existences to decide the judgment. I also want to administer the judgment. I'm the executioner, and I'm going to punish you."

However, the deed of the executioner is not a pleasant one. Have you ever noticed that when you enter into punishment, you somehow end up getting punished? That is a little wake-up signal from God. There are better things in store for you. You are a co-creator, so you are allowed to create what you choose. If you choose to be an executioner, then you assign yourself to an executioner's place. One day you may find out that you're sick and tired of the way you're executing your life to your disadvantage. You may realize that you don't have to be judge, jury, and executioner and may begin recognizing that you have better choices. You may call out to a higher form, perhaps simply saying, "Oh, God, please help me." You probably have had moments on your knees, crying out to God. **When you**

6. LUKE 6:37

are at your worst is when God is most available to you.
That is an important realization for all of us.

Here is one way to check out God and Spirit. You
may not have done this since the last time you were "down
on your knees." Bring to mind whatever you were down
on your knees about—what you were calling out for—and
look at your life since that time. Since that time, have you
moved closer to God? This does not necessarily mean you
got what you thought you wanted, and you might want to
consider that what you asked for really was not the best for
you. But if you got closer to God, then I suggest to you
that your prayer was answered and that your life has been
enriched since. **If you are looking for a criterion to dis-
cern if you are closer to God, all you really need to
consider is whether you have become more loving
toward yourself and your life in this world.**

Living a blessed life represents the process of getting
closer to God. God is already present, here and now. When
we come into the world, we move out of the awareness of
God, and we experience it as a sense of separation. To
some degree, I know you know what I'm talking about,
since part of being human is experiencing separation. To
be a Soul in the human form is to reexperience God within
you and to experience God in all things. Locating your
own inner spiritual awareness is the process of moving into
the oneness of God.

The source of God is not out in the world. It is not
like the Wizard of Oz. Some people attempt to pretend it is
like that when they go off, trying to find God sitting on a

throne somewhere, on some mountaintop, or in a cave. That is a futile search. Certainly, that approach is a search that will disillusion you.

Disillusionment is a blessing. Be thankful when your illusions are removed even if the result is falling from ivory towers or positions of recognition. If you gain the world and lose your Soul, what have you gained? Nothing. You are going to lose the world eventually anyway. It is a guaranteed, inevitable, foregone conclusion. But if you gain the Soul while losing the world, you have gained who you are.

Why try to possess something you are going to leave behind? Jesus the Christ said it clearly: "Seek ye first the kingdom of God, and his righteousness; and all these things shall be added unto you."[7] The challenge then becomes how to stay free as all the things are added unto you, lest you become caught once again in the very things that would bind you into the world.

What do we experience when we devote ourselves to seeking God first? We bring forward loving, caring, and sharing; health, wealth, and happiness; riches, abundance, and prosperity. When we entirely seek God, then God entirely blesses us. That is my experience. Don't stop short before you entirely realize God. That doesn't happen entirely until you leave this world.

In the meantime, make God's blessings so certain that they are entirely alive and full in your life. God's blessings are everywhere and in everything. God is love. **When your**

7. MATTHEW 6:33

life is full of love, your life is fully blessed. The task is to always walk the path of loving in all ways.

Baruch Bashan.

A Blessing of Grace and Loving

❧ GOD HAS A PLAN FOR YOU.

It is an insurance plan called grace.

Grace is that action of God that takes you home
   in spite of yourself,
   in spite of your conditions.

Grace is available even for those actions about which you
have said,
"I would not do that,"
and you have done it anyway,
not just once, but over and over.

In spite of it all, you can give yourself over to God
   completely—or as much as you can in each moment.
You do the best you can because God understands.
No matter where you find yourself,
   no matter what has happened,

how you got yourself into it,

how entangled it is,

how complicated, misconstrued, misconceived,

misaligned

—no matter what—

God understands,

and God's grace is always extended to you.

How do you enter into grace?

Love God.

What does that mean?

Love everything.

Just start where you are.

Start with yourself.

Isn't it amazing that it would be set up that way,

that you would begin where you are now, with yourself?

That is what you will be doing from now on,

on your way home to God.

You will realize,

"What allowed me to come home to God

is that I loved everything.

No matter what came before me,

no matter what was present,

no matter what happened,

what I did,

   or what they did,

I moved to loving,

and then I moved on."

What if your life in this world was laid out so simply

   that it required just one choice?

Just one.

And that choice is loving.

You make that choice over and over and over

until it becomes how you are in every moment.

Whenever you look upon yourself, you look upon loving.

You change your identity so that it becomes loving,

so that the only place where we can ever find you

   is loving.

You will then become God.

You will fulfill your heritage,

   your destiny,

   what you came here to do.

You will live here and in the Spirit at the same time.

The Spirit is with you, absolutely 100 percent.

It is your ally and your friend.

It is going to do everything that you need.

Call on it, and bring yourself forward to the Spirit.

Charge yourself with Spirit.

Infuse yourself with Spirit.

Live Spirit's way.

That is the way that goes through the sound of God,

    the name of God,

    the word of God.

It is openly offered to you.

It is freely given.

Are you freely choosing?

As you freely choose into the grace of God,

calling upon the name of God

    morning, noon, and night

    and every time in between,

then you infuse yourself with God.

You become one with God.

You also discover that all the conditions are blessings,

that there is no condition that is not a blessing of God,

and that who you are

is the unconditional loving of God.

Baruch Bashan.

A Blessing of Rededication

☙ FATHER-MOTHER GOD, we ask for your attunement with
     us just now.

May you bring forward the Light of higher consciousness,
     the Light of the Spirit,
     of the anointed one,
that this Light can come through each one of us,
     filling, surrounding, and protecting us,
that the Light comes in truth,
     comes as a witness to who we are.

We ask for clarification, purification, and cleansing
     of any negativity,
     any disturbance,
     on any level.

Let us be open to receive and attune,

> to release our areas of disbelief or belief,

> that we come to you open and innocent.

We're grateful for the sanctity that's placed here.

Father, once again we ask for your blessing to reach into each

> one of us,

> in our consciousness where you find us,

to guide us to your way.

Would you now assist us in releasing ourselves from those

> places we have bound ourselves?

Where we have placed restrictions or blocks,

let them be removed and released.

Bring forth your mercy,

> your forgiveness,

and turn us to your highest essence.

Let us sing your praise, knowing that your will is being done

> perfectly,

> that all is turned to good,

> and, therefore, this is a time of gladness and gratitude.

Let us be one who becomes an instrument of your will.

Let us have the desire that is of your consciousness.

Give us the strength and the resolve to carry forth these blessings,

    and let us know the courage that is of the heart,

    that we walk sturdy and firm,

    aligned with you all of our days.

Baruch Bashan.

A Prayer

I'm going to take advantage of the opportunity to speak to the Lord, and I'll just share it openly with you.

&❧ LORD, I give thanks that I know your presence, for the continuous connection that you bring, that you extend to us all very personally. I'm thankful for being part of your family in such an intimate, personal way. I'm glad to be a part of this work that goes on, that extends out to all those who are looking for this consciousness that you are and all the special ways that we manage to do the world.

I ask that we each be strengthened in our knowing of this connection and that it goes out in this day, to this year, throughout our entire life, preparing the way and blessing us. We each can release ourselves from whatever temptations might befall us and place ourselves into the renewed knowing, the understanding of what you are doing with us and what we are doing with you.

I ask this blessing to extend to all those who are in the Traveler's fold, that they are awakened in their own way. I give thanks for the perfection of how it is all done, how it's revealed and not revealed, how it is known absolutely in Spirit and how it is a mystery in this world. I give thanks for the ordinariness that places your presence as God, that we may know it in the flesh.

I ask that we may be renewed, bringing forth a new aliveness and vitality in the Spirit, that the new experiences of joy and rejoicing come forward and that we be a people, a family, a community that rejoices in the Spirit and demonstrates the presence for all. And I ask that we be lifted in grace.

So be it.

Baruch Bashan.

MORE BLESSINGS

Many of the blessings in this book were excerpted from the greater body of John Morton's work. And you may have noticed that some of John's other works, such as audio and video tapes, were done in conjunction with John-Roger (J-R). The explanation for this is simple and interesting.

The work that John Morton and J-R do is an expression of a spiritual consciousness called the Mystical Traveler. The blessings and teachings come from that source, and both John and J-R have their own unique way of presenting this special information.

If you've enjoyed this book, you may want to explore the teachings more deeply through the Movement of Spiritual Inner Awareness (MSIA), where John Morton serves as Spiritual Director. We suggest the following resources listed on the next page.

SOUL AWARENESS DISCOURSES—A HOME STUDY COURSE FOR YOUR SPIRITUAL GROWTH

The heart of John-Roger's teachings, Soul Awareness Discourses provide a structured and methodical approach to gaining greater awareness of ourselves and our relationship to the world and to God. Each year's study course contains twelve lessons, one for each month. Discourses offer a wealth of practical keys to more successful living. Even more, they provide keys to greater spiritual knowledge and awareness of the Soul.

$100 one-year subscription
To order call MSIA at 323/737-4055

SOUL AWARENESS TAPE (SAT) SERIES

These audio tapes provide a new talk by John-Roger every month on a variety of topics, ranging from practical living to spiritual upliftment. In addition, SAT subscribers may purchase previous SAT releases.

$100 one-year subscription
To order call MSIA at 323/737-4055

LOVING EACH DAY

Loving Each Day is a daily e-mail message from MSIA that contains an uplifting quote or passage from John Morton or John-Roger, intended to inspire the reader and give them pause to reflect on the Spirit within. Loving Each Day is available in four languages—English, Spanish, French and Portuguese.

A subscription is free upon request.

To subscribe, please visit the web site www.msia.org

We welcome your comments and questions. Contact us at

MSIA

P.O. Box 513935

Los Angeles, CA 90051-1935

323/737-4055

soul@msia.org

www.msia.org

حرف و گفت و صوت را بر هم زنم   تا که بی این هر سه با تو دم زنم

رومی

"*I*'m going to throw away sound, talk, and formal things,
so that *I* can communicate with you on another plane."

تاله بی این هم سه پا بودم رقم رون